Van

The History and Tips to Recognize a Real Vampire

(Essays on the Undead in Popular Culture Around the World)

Wanda Johnson

Published By **Phil Dawson**

Wanda Johnson

All Rights Reserved

Vampires: The History and Tips to Recognize a Real Vampire (Essays on the Undead in Popular Culture Around the World)

ISBN 978-1-77485-531-7

No part of this guidebook shall be reproduced in any form without permission in writing from the publisher except in the case of brief quotations embodied in critical articles or reviews.

Legal & Disclaimer

from and against any damages, costs, and expenses, including any legal fees potentially resulting from the application of any of the information provided by this guide. This disclaimer applies to any damages or injury caused by the use and application, whether directly or indirectly, of any advice or information presented, whether for breach of contract, tort, negligence, personal injury, criminal intent, or under any other cause of action.

You agree to accept all risks of using the information presented inside this book. You need to consult a professional medical practitioner in order to ensure you are both able and healthy enough to participate in this program.

Table of Contents

Introduction

The Vampire by Edvard Munch

The human race has always been scared about the deceased. Since the dawn of humankind humans have cared for the deceased and tried to keep them from coming back. There are many stories and myths regarding the return of the dead among most popular ones is the tale of the vampire.

The werewolves have been a popular part of culture. Through the 19th century and the in the 20th century there was a myriad of novels, plays and films that featured people who transformed into wolves or humanoids , and went on a rampage. The werewolf mythology is so commonplace that the people of the globe are aware of the mythology and mythology that they transform the full moon is only stopped by silver. They also transmit the disease through bites on their victims.

Actually, these beliefs weren't originally part of folklore about werewolves and were embellished later by artists. Lycanthropy's belief is much more ancient and complex than many people imagine that it dates back to antiquity. werewolves were once believed to be real. Indeed, many were tried and then executed for it because justice system was convinced they could alter their appearance and murder innocent people. For hundreds decades, the werewolves were a symbol of an odd and ancient custom that continues to resonate in the society until today.

In the same way, although everybody has been told about vampires, only a many are not aware of the mythology and folklore that created the mythical creatures so well-known. In fact, there are so numerous legends and stories from many cultures that it's difficult to determine the exact meaning, and folklore is, by nature nonscientific. However, most folks within the Western world see vampires as being creatures that return from the dead to steal blood or the essence of life from the living.

This popular understanding of vampires obscures a lot of European and non-European beliefs of blood sucking monsters. For instance In China, Japan, and the Middle East, there are spirits that take the life force out of the unwary However, these supernatural beings weren't real humans. According to African or Native American traditions, there are monsters who perform the same thing although they are believed to be from this Earth however, they are not human beings.

Additionally, the folklore of the time changes with time, meaning that the vampires that we know in the present (and those that some claim to have met) have little in common with the vampires of the early modern Europe. Stories evolve, fiction transforms into fact, and vice versa, and the underlying beliefs are continually re-invented. As an example, we have this exhilarating account in on the 20th October 1855 issue of Middlesex Illustrated Times titled "A Story about a Vampire":

"A German paper relates a interesting instance of this popular belief that was recently observed in Spalato in Dalmatia:

"A beautiful and young girl born to wealthy peasants, had many potential suitors, and she picked one from her own affluence. Their bethrothal as a couple was marked with a lavish feast which was arranged to the daughter's dad. At midnight, the daughter and her mother retreated to their bedroom with their father, and left the guests at the table. At once, the women were heard screaming horribly, and then the second following, the mother, thin and pale, ran into the room, dragging her daughter in her arms and crying with an inexplicable voice of sorrow"A vampire! a vampire ! my daughter has passed away "

"The village doctor was among the guests. He saw that the girl only fainted, gave her a cordial which brought her back to consciousness and then he asked her. She said that while she was getting dressed the night before, a spectre of pale light, covered in a shroud came in through the window, attacked her and then smacked her on the neck. then he disappeared. She added that she recognized the man as

4

Krysnewsky who was a rejected lover of hers who had passed away a fortnight prior to.

"The doctor tried to convince her that she could be a victim of a delusion but she refused to give up on her tale. The parents and the guests were convinced that she was actually bit by a vampire and were extremely angry at the doctor for assuming to claim otherwise.

"The following day, nearly all of the males in the town, all armed and women, went to the graveyard, shouting terrible curses against Krysnewsky, the vampire. Krysnewsky. The body for the decedent was pulled up, and then was forced to open. Then, being lifted to the top 20 guns were fired on the head of the body. The skull's fragments were taken away, and then, in the midst of wild dances and cries were smoldering in a massive fire, and so the body was later.

"The girl was found to be seriously ill and was ill over the course of a fortnight before she passed away. She would always insist she had been bit into the neck by vampires however, she refused to on any reason allow the doctor look at the wound. After her death she was able to remove the bandages off her neck and discovered an insignificant wound on her throat that had the appearance of being created by an awl made by a harness maker which was poisoned. The doctor later learned that the people who rejected the love interest to the woman was actually a maker of harnesses from a nearby village and he believed that the person responsible was the one who attacked the girl. He provided information to officials, and the man, when he heard that he was going to be detained, fled to the mountains and took his own life by slithering into the river."

Researcher for vampires Rob Brautigam has discovered that this story was reprinted with a few minor changes from a work of fiction written by French novelist Prosper Merimee. However, this plagiarism that is presented as factual demonstrates the fundamental nature of folklore. Ideas are adapted, adopted and presented as truthful. While all the while the myth of the vampire is not forgotten.

Chapter 1: Ancient Vampires

The vampires the world knows today are just as an invention of popular books or Hollywood like they are the result of the early folklore. The works by Bram Stoker and a string of other writers and film makers have nothing to do with the mythological origins of the creature. For instance, the idea that vampires must return to the coffin each day isn't often found in folklore. Likewise, even though vampires are known to go back to the grave after removing the victim's blood but it's not required to visit the grave. In reality, Bram Stoker came up this idea to restrict Dracula's movements and to give his hero a chance to be able to kill him. In the same way, vampires frequently roam around during daylight hours and include Stoker's Dracula and the notion of the vampires being destroyed by sunlight is rooted in the silent film Nosferatu produced by F.W. Murnau. The legendary German director wanted to put a dramatic ending to his monster and was caught at sunrise and in which the creature from the night vanishes. In later films and novels the idea was re-imagined by making the vampire age quickly or even burn before transforming into ashes.

Bela Lugosi as Dracula

A photo taken from Nosferatu

The legend of the vampire that these fictional depictions take their inspiration from originates in Eastern Europe in the Late Middle Ages and depicts the body of a deceased person who rose from their grave to draw vital energy or blood of the living. The vampire did this by gnawing in the neck, or on other areas of the body. It also did this attacking victims in different ways, but in some cases all it did in order to drain the life force out of the living was lay on one of them. The victims of the vampire would usually die and the vampire would cause a rash of pestilence to kill those it had not directly targeted.

The word "vampire" is from Eastern European origin. It is stated in the Oxford English Dictionary specifies that it's Slavonic, "occurring in the same way with respect to Russian, Polish, Czech, Serbian, and Bulgarian including variants such like Bulgarian vapir, the word vepir, Ruthenian vepyr, vopyr and opyr. Russian upir, upyrand Polish upior." These variants could originate of that of the Turkish word uber which is a reference to a witch. In the Turkish Ottoman Empire ruled the majority the region of Eastern Europe, and its influence on culture had a vast spread.

Although some of the particulars of the mythology of the vampire originate from Eastern Europe, the idea of a demon, or ghost (sometimes of a deceased or deceased person) sucking the life-essence out of a living person is a relic from the past. The Indian Sanskrit legend of Baital-Pachisi originally written in 1037, but likely dating back to earlier, there's the creature known as Baital. Baital Spirit that could make dead people appear like they're alive. The Baital hangs on a tree upside down as bats. The famous adventurer as well as Orientalist Sir Richard Francis Burton translated the text into English He retitled the text Vikram The Vampire and Vikram. In the late 19th century, vampires held an influence in people's English imagination.

Burton

In the past, in Greece and Rome there was several creatures with vampiric traits. The famous Occult historian Montague Summers was a prolific writer trying to establish that vampires existed throughout Classical Greece and Rome, but he acknowledged "I believe that the idea of vampiric existed in the majority of ancient peoples. The only major difference, that is significant but not necessarily essential is that while the real vampire is dead and the vampires of older beliefs were usually ghosts or spectres, however they were ghosts who were often tangible, as well as spectres that were able to cause serious harm to people living by consuming their vitality and drained the blood of their victims." (Summers 1926).

A more apt parallel to the classic vampire is a tale from the old Celtic mythology. A wizard known as Abhartach believed that his wife was having a relationship with a woman who was not true, so he was able to hide on a ledge just outside the bedroom of his wife. He fell down, and since the wizard was famous and was buried straight in the customary manner of burials for the kings. The next day, he showed up at the settlement and instructed all the residents to cut off their wrists and then bleed into a bowl that he carried in order to consume the blood to speak and walk as a normal human being. Many times, the locals employed killers to eliminate the wizard, but he always came back. Then a druid decided to rid the creature. He made a sword out of yew, pushed it through Abhartach's body, laid him upside down, afterward, covered Abhartach's grave with ash leaves as well as thorns and an enormous boulder. The druid warned Abhartach was not likely to be killed, which is why Abhartach is still in his grave, waiting for unsuspecting travellers to wander too close, so Abhartach can grab them.

Other northern European religions have also been believed to believe in the power of wizards to make the living dead. One example is the Norse Aptrgongumenn that were raised from the dead by a wizard who did his orders. In order to kill the creature, one needed take off the head of it and its foot, and place its head at the top of the leg, and the foot at the top of neck. Runes with binding were usually placed on grave markers to prevent wizards from raising an person. If a wicked wizard passed away, he would turn into a kind of revenant, known as Drauge. Drauges could steal the vitality of a person just by looking at them. The tomb was not able to be left however, and the Drauge was easily avoided by everyone except tomb thieves. Indeed, the numerous old myths about the vengeful bodies attacking people who went into tombs might be a method to stop grave robbers.

Chapter 2: Early Werewolf Legends

Although the legend of the werewolf didn't fully develop up to the Late Middle Ages in Europe The history of the legend can be traced back to its beginnings all way back to the beginning of time. The notion of a human changing into the wild is a long-standing one, closely linked to many of the oldest myths. It is possibly a record of our own evolutionary journey from simpler animals or perhaps the human's innate fascination with and fear of our natural surroundings. In the end, our modern-day disconnect from nature is not a new thing, and for the majority of the human race's history, people lived in close proximity to nature, and predators like the wolf were a real danger. In the context of history was a natural one, people worried that by some kind of magic they could turn their neighbors into wild animals.

The early Indo-European mythology had numerous instances of warriors wearing animal skins to emulate the characteristics of animals. They were usually predators like the bear or the wolf. Shamans also did this to channel the spirit animal in order to connect with the world that is not visible. These ancient legends and representations don't show shamans or warriors becoming bears or wolves. It is a mental or spiritual change and not physical.

The first real transformations are found in the writings that is written in Classical Greece and Rome, where certain sources refer to transformations in shape as a real fact. It is believed that the Greek writers Herodotus (c. 484-425 BCE) wrote in his renowned work Histories of an Central Asian tribe called the Neuri who were all transformed into wolves every year for a period of several days.

fifth century BCE Greek representation of Dolon wearing a wolf's costume at the time of the Trojan War

Others Classical writers were not convinced. For instance, in Natural History, Pliny the Elder (23-79 CE) wrote, "That men have been transformed into wolves, and later returned to their former shape, is something we can consider as untrue or, in fact, we're ready to believe in all the myths that, over many centuries were found to be fascinating. Butthe idea of it is very ingrained in the minds of ordinary people that it may cause the expression "Versipellis" ["changing one's skin"which is now commonly used as a type of imprecation. I'll be pointing out the source of it. Euanthes, one of the Grecian writer of a reputable fame, explains that the Arcadians claim that an individual belonging to the family of Anthus is chosen by a lot and taken to a particular lake in this region, where, after hanging his clothes on an oak tree, he swam across the lake and then disappears to the desert. There, it is transformed into a wolf , and then reunites with other animals belonging to similar species over a period that is nine years. If he's able to prevent him from seeing a man throughout that period, he comes back to the lake and, upon swimming across it, reverts to his normal appearance, just adding nine years to his appearance. To this, Fabius states that he still wears his previous clothes too. It's amazing to see just how far the skepticism of the Greeks will stretch! There isn't a lie even if it is a bit barefaced and they cannot be proved to be the truth."

Other stories described the gods transforming men into wolves as the consequence of a crime. In Metamorphoses the epic work by Ovid, the Roman poem Ovid (43 BCE - 17/18 CE) There is an account of Lycaon manipulating Jupiter to eat human flesh. When the god's king realized the trick Lycaon did He was angry and transformed Lycaon to the form of a animal.

A drawing depicting Zeus changing Lycaon into the form of a Wolf

It seems that even though the concept of a human transformation into a wolf an everyday occurrence in these ancient societies but it was believed to be a different thing from the normal existence. That is, people who were capable of transformation either resided in remote locations or awaited the divine intervention. The more educated people of society were skeptical of the tales in any way. This would change by the Late Middle Ages, when werewolves were widely accepted by a greater percentage of the population as a fact.

Prior to this however, the foundation was being prepared in various Germanic and Slavic culture to support the same belief. The details are hazy and are found through scattered references however they do hint at a larger system of belief. For instance In a few Norse stories, Harald Fairhair, the King Harald Fairhair of Norway (c. 850-932) was a member of an army of elite soldiers referred to as Ulfhednar ("wolf covered") The individuals wore the pelts animals and channeled the spirit and ferocity of animals during combat. They were akin to the famous berserkers who wore bear hides, for similar reasons. These kinds of warriors were famous for their ability to sustain many wounds that could be fatal to an average person, and still fight. They would often fall to death after combat had concluded.

A drawing depicts Odin being pursued by an erserker

The Slavs also shared tales of animals similar to contemporary perceptions of werewolves. In The Tale of Igor's Campaign, an epic poem of ambiguous source that many scholars attribute to the 13th century recounts the exploits of the prince who was a historical figure, Igor Svyatoslavich The Brave (1151-1201/1202) who was a ruler from the Rus. The poem also speaks of another prince from the past, Vseslav of Polotsk (c. 1039-1101). The poem depicts him as an individual in the day and a wolf during evening, capable of travelling long lengths of distances "Vseslav was the Prince who ruled people; as a the prince, he was in charge of towns; however, at night, he swam disguised as the Wolf. From Kiev and prowling at night, he landed, in front of the crew of the cock, Tmutorokan. The way of Great Sun like the wolf that prowled, crossed. He was in Polotsk they rang at the time of matins earlier at St. Sophia the bells however he could hear the bells ringing within Kiev."

Werewolves also appeared in several early modern and medieval geography. Olaus Magnus (1490-1557) Archbishop of Uppsala and prolific writer included these words in his A Description of Northern Peoples:

"In Prussia, Livonia, and Lithuania however, the people suffer greatly from the ferocity of wolves during the entire year, as they eat their cattle and scatter them throughout the forest whenever they wander off in the minimum, but this isn't viewed as a problem as serious in comparison to the suffering they suffer from humans who are transformed into wolves.

"On the celebration on that of the Nativity of Christ in the midnight, a crowd of wolves changed from humans are gathered in a particular location, and are arranged in a group and spread out to rage with incredible fierceness against humans as well as animals that aren't wild, and that those living in these regions are more affected by them than from natural and genuine animals, for when human presence is discovered by them, and they are confined to forests, they attack the place with a ferocious attack, attempting to destroy the doorways, and in the event that they do that, they eat all humans, as well as all animals that are found inside. They break into the beer cellars and empty the beer tuns or mead, then pile them on top of each other within the basement, making clear their differences from the genuine and natural wild wolves ... In between Lithuania, Livonia, and Courland are the walls of an ancient castle that has been destroyed. In this area, thousands of people gather at a time and test their agility in leaping. If they are not able to leap across the wall, as happens often for the fattest, get being slapped with scourges by the captains, and killed."

A scholar named Samuel Rhanaeus, who was active during the second half during the late 17th century wrote extensively about werewolves:

"There are a myriad of instances which are not simply based on sources, but from solid evidence for us to doubt the reality that Satan, if we don't doubt that a supernatural being exists and does his work through the dark children--has

Lycanthropists within his web in three ways:3.

"1. They perform as wolves specific actions, for example, the capture of a sheep, killing cattle, etc. They are not transformed into wolves, as nobody in the scientific community in Courland believes, however, they do so in their human frames and using their human limbs, but in that they are in a state of phantasy or hallucination, they think they are transformed into wolves and are considered to be wolves by those who suffer from similar hallucinations, and as a result, they run these people as wolves in packs even though they are not real wolves.

"2. They think, while in deep sleep, or during a dream that they hurt the animals, and do the whole thing without ever getting off their couch however their master will do, on their behalf according to what their imaginations point out or suggests to him.

"3. The evil one causes natural wolves to commit an action, and then retells it so clearly to the sleeper, and remains to his spot at night, as well as upon awakening, that he believes that the action to have been done by himself."

In time, a set of beliefs was formed around the idea of the werewolf and lycanthropes were incorporated into the folklore. Similar to all folklores particular beliefs differed between regions however there was a common beliefs throughout Europe. However in the same vein as the quote earlier, there were those who doubted the idea of shapeshifting and instead saw Lycanthropy as a kind of madness caused by either the Devil or simply.

The majority of werewolves were men, however, it was only Finland as well as Scandinavia where the vast majority of werewolves were thought to be female. They were in those areas more like witches with deadly claws that could curse children and livestock by their eerie eyes.

The transformation of the werewolf was typically only temporary, changing to hunt in the evening, then changing back to hunt to become an ordinary citizen. Another belief was that the werewolf changed for a period of time, perhaps weeks or days. In a few stories it was said that the change would last for a long time as was the bipedal werewolf in literature and films was invented later on.

The werewolf of old would usually transform to a wolf, which was undistinguishable from a normal wolf, in terms of size, its fierceness and, in a few stories, its eyes. Sometimes, it did not have the tail. In some instances humans did not change at all, but simply got up on four legs and ran around as if an Wolf. While the animals often chased after live victims (mostly likely that the majority of these were genuine wolf attacks) They were also recognized for digging into the graves of deceased people and then eat their decaying corpses.

One of the most interesting cases came from Paris in 1848. In the fall of that year many cemeteries were broken into with bodies being separated and smashed to pieces. At first , the guards believed it was an animal However, in one location, they discovered footprints of a human within the soft earth. The defilement slowed down for a few minutes, and after which it resumed. Nobody could identify the culprit or understand the reason why anyone would be so shrewd.

In March of the year following the perpetrator was into trouble. The watchmen put up an automatic spring gun, which was a shotgun that was fired via a tripwire, and is commonly employed to kill poachers and also on grave defilers. Nearby neighbors of to the burial ground in S. Parnasse heard the gun fire one night, and the watchmen ran to find out if the elusive person was actually killed. As the arrival of their team, they witnessed an officer in uniform leap across the wall nearby and disappear.

A smudge of blood and a ripped piece of uniform proved that the man was shot and the police went to every local barracks to find a person suffering from a gunshot injury. They discovered the victim an officer from the 1st Regiment named Bertrand. When he was tried, he confessed to the crime, stating that the desire to slander the dead swept upon him on a rainy day in the month of February in 1847. He was walking in the vicinity of the church when a sudden rainstorm prompted him to run to the holy church. In the church, he observed that the grave of a woman's remains inside the churchyard hadn't been properly lined up. The spade was right next to it and he felt an

26

overwhelming urge to attack the body of the deceased.

He offered this explanation

"Soon I lifted the corpse from the grave and began to smear it up with the spade but not really being aware of what I was doing. A worker saw me as I laid on the ground until the labourer was gone and then threw the corpse back to the grave. I then walked away and washed myself in cold sweat, and went to an enclave in which I lay for a while, notwithstanding the freezing rain that came down, and in a state exhausted to the point of exhaustion. As I awoke in the morning, my limbs felt like they were broken and my head was was weak. The same sensation and prostration came with every attack.

"Two days later I was back in the cemetery I opened up the tombstone using my hands. My hands were bleeding but I did not feel the pain. Instead, I ripped the body to pieces and threw it back to the hole."

The attack continued after the first attack, and the attacker regularly targeted females' bodies of all ages, from toddlers to older women, at times cutting the body in pieces and then putting it in the mud. Sometimes, he'd cut the body in pieces by using a spade as during his first attack. In other instances, he would rip the body apart using the fingers of his mouth or his fingernails.

Bertrand was well-known for his bouts of melancholy and said that those, which were often fuelled by long periods of drinking wine, would often trigger the intense impulses. Bertrand never planned his actions and acted only at the spur of the moment, and would be in an exhaustion state afterward. This was a normal occurrence of the werewolves who were believed to be exhausted by their battles. Although the media branded him as a monster, he wasn't punished for being a werewolf like the werewolf would surely be two centuries earlier. Instead, he was sentenced to one year in jail and a very small penalty for someone evidently criminally insane.

There were many different versions of beliefs in Europe believed that in human form the werewolf exhibited signs of his disease and that meant there were a variety of ways to recognize the presence of a werewolf. They usually had a unibrow long, curly and thick nails, ears that were set low on the sides on the top of their heads, as well as a smooth swinging stride that resembled the animal's. Some traditions also said that children that were born without hair, or the caul would be shape-shifters. In the next section, certain tribes were famous for having a high number of werewolves, including the Neuri and the Livonians along with the Transdanubians.

In numerous stories there are stories where the wolf was wounded by a brave hunter, or a potential victim. when the werewolf reverted back to human form, they'd remain with the injury. A suspected werewolf who was in human form could be cut and fur would protrude through the wound. In Russia it was believed that werewolves had fur on its tongue.

The notion that a werewolf bite can transmit lycanthropy is a new concept that is used in the majority of court instances, it was believed that the werewolf acquired its power via an arrangement in a deal with the Devil and indirectly by one or more of devil's minions on Earth. The concept of a wolfskin cape , or the wolf belt that allowed the wearer to alter through the ages until the 17th century. However, at that time, it was seen not as a mere trick, but also a signifying Satan's demons, as all magic was believed to be an act by the Devil.

The way Richard Verstegan wrote in his 1628 treatise, A Remembrance of Decayed Intelligence "[Thereare] certayne sorcerers who, after afflicting them with an ointment they create by the whims of the devil and then putting on an inchaunted girdle that does not only in the eyes of others appear like wolves, but in their own mind, they have the appearance and the nature of wolves as long they are wearing the girdle. They also behave as wolves in the killing and squabbling the majority of humans."

There are also said as magical rivers, and no doubt, they were holy during pre-Christian times, in which people could bathe and gain the strength. The people could also drink the rainwater that was left by a wolf's footprint.

The connection to the full moon with werewolves a tinny one. The only evidence of a direct connection in the literature of folklore is to be found in Germany and France where people were able to get the power during certain summer nights by sleeping outdoors by the light of the moon upon their faces. It's interesting to observe that this induced the condition of lycanthropy but they were not required to switch their clothes every full moon.

The cure for a werewolf was a difficult matter. In the past, in Greece and Rome there was a belief that forcing those suffering from the disease to exercise vigorously until they fell down would heal the condition. Of of course that to those that were demented and believed the world was a wolf, that might alleviate their symptoms for a short period of time however one must be curious about what ancient doctors did after the patient had stopped and his delusion had returned.

The werewolf was a threat to the Christian faith. Christian times, as the werewolf who was suspected of being a threat was thought to have signed a contract with Satan and Satan, remedies were not often considered. In most cases, the werewolf was punished with the same punishment that witches receive which was burns at stake. The courts that were more compassionate attempted exorcism, or in Germany cutting nails through the palms, in imitation of Christ's suffering. Christ.

A little further north to the north of Schleswig-Holstein The werewolves got off fairly easily. All one needed to do was name the werewolf the Christian names three times before they would be back in their human form and never to change.

There were very few instances where was there silver or a bullet made of silver employed against the werewolf. However, there is a legend dating back to the 19th century from Devonshire concerning two huge black hounds who came off the moors, and regularly drank of the local cider at an inn nearby. The proprietor of the inn, when he finally pulled out the strength to confront the frightening beasts, put the silver button on their heads. At this the two hounds changed into two elderly women who lived in the nearby area. Naturally, this story seems to be more of the story of witchcraft rather instead of Lycanthropy.

The greatest care had to be taken when disposing of the werewolf's corpse this is the reason why people accused of being werewolves are usually burned or dismembered. This was in the event that this wasn't done, it was believed that they could return to life as werewolves. For instance, in Poland and Germany there was a belief that the remains of big sinners would turn into wolves at night , to feast on the living, and then revert back to corpses during the day which is an intriguing mix of vampire and werewolf mythologies.

Further to the east, in a region where belief of vampires were prevalent there is a deeper connection. In Greece the person who suffers from lycanthropy can fall into a state of trance, where his soul departs his body, enters the animal's body, and wanders around in search of drinking blood. If it returns it is exhausted. When the lycanthrope is dead the body, it returns as the vampire.

In Serbia the vampires and werewolves are known in the same way, Vlkoslak and they infest the countryside during the winter months. They also organize large gatherings during which they remove their wolf skins and dance about with one another. If someone can locate one of the skins that is burned, the Vlkoslak would be treated.

The Russians call the werewolf wawkalak. It is when a person becomes one by wrathing the Devil and then being cursed by the Dark One. The person is transformed into a wolf, and runs from house to home soliciting for food from his family members. The wolf is innocent however, he is terribly trapped in the form it is and forced to move around from the place to another.

Chapter 3: Vampire Traits

An examination of the old folklore, in both oral histories as well as written reports shows a wide range in the stories of vampires, but this shouldn't be a surprise. Up until the middle of the twentieth century Eastern Europe consisted mostly of small towns with no large cities, and most people lived in small, isolated villages from the other people in the world. They rarely traveled and, as a result, common beliefs were influenced by local customs as stories were passed from generation on to the following generation.

The story's basic premise is that a person in the community would pass away in the midst of the night, and soon thereafter, the community would suffer a succession of other deaths, most often from the family members of the deceased. The deceased was believed to be vampires, and was believed to have returned from the grave to steal the life-force from the living. This could be due to various reasons. The person may have committed suicide or lived an unholy life, and when the body is exhumed, it is discovered to be brimming with apparent vitality. The belly is filled with blood, blood is visible in the mouth, cheeks are glowing, and the limbs are flexible. The body is often been moved into the coffin, and it's no longer lying on its back, flat with arms at the side, but instead flipped to the side, with legs and arms bent. A stake is pushed through the chest of the vampire, and the body emits an intense scream, which is another sign that it's one of the dead.

It is crucial to remember that in the folklore of the beginning vampires never actually left their graves. Since the majority of suspected vampires were peasants they didn't have a coffin in the first place , since they were typically buried in shrouds. The body remains underground while the spirit of the vampire walks through the ground.

In other stories where the vampire is magically transform into a vampire and disappear through a small gap close to its grave. Additionally, the vampire seldom suckers blood from the neck. If it does suck blood typically, it does so via the chest. In some mythologies such as those found in Arab and Persian regions the vampire is said to suckle blood through the big toe of the victim's. A lot of European vampire myths depict the vampire sucking life's essence of the victim by lying on the victim and putting an oppressive pressure on the chest of the victim.

Vampires can cause more than this. They may be the poltergeists who throw objects about, consuming all the alcohol and food within a home or farm, and even infiltrating holy sites. A few stories suggest that the creature doesn't cause any harm to anyone or even hurts them, it's more of a terrifying nuisance as predators.

In a serious way the belief was that vampires were carriers of disease. One of the first vampire myths that circulate in Europe is about Berwick, the Berwick vampire. In the year 1196 an unsavory merchant was killed by disease in the town of Berwick that was located situated in England or Scotland according to the source. This could be a misguided reference to Berwick-upon-Tweed which is a town located that lies between England and Scotland that was changed hands several times during the Middle Ages before the two nations were joined. The town was laid to rest in unhallowed grounds due to his petty sins and was soon back to be a recurring threat to the living. He would show up like a decaying corpse in the midnight, and scurry through the streets, screaming, "Until my body is burnt, the inhabitants of Berwick will not be able to rest in tranquility!" Shortly after his appearance, half of the population had died of disease, so survivors were able to dig him up and removed his limbs and head and then burned his body until nothing was left.

The fear of spreading contagion is a theme throughout a lot of tales about vampires. The vampire is usually the first person to die from an outbreak, and thus blamed for deaths that follow. Although this is a fundamental notion from the past of spreading of diseases, it's changed into something far more sinister when it is believed that it is an intentional decision by the dead.

There are local variations that say that vampires may be created through other methods, like being victimized by a vampire, seeing a cat walk across the grave of a person as well as being cursed or rejected by parents or witches. There are many traditions that say that if one eats the meat taken from an animal killed by an wolf, they be transformed into a vampire. One type of German vampire, known as Blutsauger. Blutsauger is one who carries dirt from the grave of its victim and puts it into the mouth of the victim. If the victim eats it, they'll be transformed into the bloody Blutsauger.

People are at risk of becoming vampires. This could result from a myriad of indications like the fact that you were born with a crown, born with teeth or being the seventh child (especially when a parent was also a seventh-child) or having a variety of defects, or even being cursed from birth. One instance of being cursed at birth is the myth about The Children of Judas. The direct descendents of Judas Iscariot were believed to lurk throughout Bulgaria, Serbia, and Romania and wore the same red hair that the tradition claims Judas was blessed with. If they assault anyone and leave a mark that bears the Roman numeral thirty (XXX). This is the same as the silver pieces that Judas received for committing a crime against Jesus.

Life-long actions can result in the rise of vampires after the person dies. This usually happens due to a criminal act, like alcoholism or suicide, leaving the church as an unkind or odd person or being a wealthy miser, or other uncivil behavior.

The proper care must be taken after the deceased person has passed away to stop them from returning. If proper funeral arrangements are performed, or if there's not enough mourning time the body could unleash revenge. It is believed that in both Eastern Europe and China, it is believed that a corpse could reanimate when a particular animal jumps over it. The type of animal is dependent on the location, and can range to a black chicken to the cat and (in Romania) a bat. This is among the rare instances in mythology of bats being linked with vampirism. It is mostly the work by writers of fiction. However, it isn't it a surprise that bats are included on the list of Romanian vampirism causes because some sources say that anything living, even a candle moving over the body could give it life.

A vampire bat

The phenomenon of vampirism appears to have hit its highest point within Eastern Europe in the late 17th and 18th centuries with numerous reports of cases throughout the region. This led to the first systematic research into vampirism done by theologians and scholars, most of whom took the information as truthful and tried to develop theories based on science and religion of the dead coming back to the world of. A number of learned treatises were published during this time along with more popular stories which is where them that a lot of the current understanding of the folklore of vampire originates.

There are some significant differences between the traditional vampire and the one that is made by films and fiction. For instance, although numerous traditions claim that the vampire is able to transform into many forms but the bat is nearly never ever mentioned. Furthermore only a few mythologies refer to the vampire having fangs. The majority of them have normal teeth, however, there is a Lampir. Lampir from Serbia, Montenegro, and Bosnia has seven fangs. Four of them are on the top row , and three at the bottom row. The Lampir and the other vampires are known to take liquid from their chests area, closest to where the heart is. On the other hand, some vampires do not suckle blood at all, instead they simply make their victims fear them or even destroy objects. In the Carpathian Mountains, the Mahr located in the Carpathian Mountains transforms into a moth, and nibbles at the victim, taking part of their soul every time they bite. When a victim is attacked, it is more vulnerable and the moth of the vampire will return till the victim's soul has been eaten. This less well-known creature is among the few vampires believed to get destroyed in the sun.

Some vampires are ruthless in their sexual cravings and will consume its victims of energy the night with sexual sex, similar to the succubus and the incubus. One common belief that is prevalent in various regions in Eastern Europe is that a male vampire would return to his wife and seek to be a part of her. If she accepts him she'll be pregnant and have a child that may one day turn out to be the vampire, or in certain traditions or legends, a vampire hunter.

Although most vampires appear only in the evening, it's not an absolute norm. In the case of Strigoi of Romania is an example. It makes its way to the grave twice per day, both at 12 noon and 12 midnight, in order to satisfy its desire for blood. In its grave, it'll be chewing on the shroud of its burial and lay in the blood pool from the victims.

The vampire graves can be identified using a variety of ways. In Romania which is the center of the vampire nation There is a belief that a small gap is always found close to the burial site of the vampire. It's the hole that which the creature makes to go in the grave and get out, miraculously shrinking in size to pass through. The hole is usually believed to be "the dimension of a snake" which refers to the Biblical symbolism of Satan with the snake. Another method to locate the burial place of a vampire is to take with a white horse across the tomb. If the animal does not respond this, it's an indication of an undead vampire underneath.

Vampires can cause all kinds of trouble beyond killing people. Similar to witches, they also destroy crops and cause bad weather. Actually, anyone studying of the folklore of witchcraft will find several similarities between witches as well as vampires. Folklorists continue to explore the reason why the Anglo-Germanic societies were more focused on witches (and therefore harmed real living people believed to be witches) and the Slavic culture was terrified of vampires that caused the same chaos and therefore killed corpses.

Greece is renowned for its belief in vampires. There was a myriad of the. The most well-known is called the Burkulakas that can be caused when someone is killed by suicide, is killed or simply suffers the misfortune of seeing cats leap over the grave of their loved one. Living people can transform into the Burkulakas when they eat the flesh of an animal that has been killed by the Wolf.

The Burkulakas is not distinct from a living being apart from it's skin pulling as tight like the drum's skin and, if someone hits the creature, it emits the identical sound of an actual drum. It'll walk all night around the village knocking on doors, and calling to residents in the name of however, it will only knock one time before it moves on. Therefore, it is a custom that is practiced in Greece not to respond to when knocked on the first time. Some scholars believe this is the reason for the belief that vampires aren't allowed to cross through the door without having been asked. If anyone is foolish enough to respond the Burkulakas invitation will be the ones to witness the vampire lie on top of them, pound them to death, then take their blood.

Believers in this, and other forms of vampires was prevalent well into the 20th century. certain researchers have blamed it due to that of the Greek Orthodox Church which was less effective in eradicating these beliefs than those of the Catholic Church. But, in the beginning of the 19th century there were some members of the church who did not approve of these kinds of things. In his book of 1835 Travels in Northern Greece, William Martin Leake writes this humorous story:

"It it would be difficult to come across an instance that is the most cruel of these beliefs, which is the one associated with the Vrukolaka. The name, Illyric appears to absolve from the Greeks of the idea, that was likely introduced to the nation by barbarians of the Slavonic race. Tournefort's description has been proven to be accurate. The Devil is said to be a part of the Vrukolaka and, upon emerging from his grave, afflicts first his closest family members and later others, leading to their deaths or losing their health. The solution is to excise the body. If, after being removed by the Priest, the demon is able to get the attention of those who live, to slice the body into tiny pieces or, if this is not enough, burn the body.

"The Metropolitan bishop of Larissa recently informed me that as a was the metropolitan of Grevena was in Grevena, he received advice from a papas who dismembered two bodies and then thrown them into the Haliacmon in the pretense of being Vrukolakas. After being summoned to the bishop's office, the priest acknowledged the truth, and claimed to justify the claim, that there was a report of an enormous animal being observed to emerge, complete by flames, from the grave in which two bodies were laid to rest. The bishop started by asking that the priest pay 250 piastres (his reverence did not mean that he gave the money to the less fortunate). He then arranged for scissors to trim the priest's beard (an inconceivable insultand was happy by scaring the priest. Then, by distributing all over the diocese that any offence similar to the one he had committed could be punished by double the fine , and a certain loss of authority the bishop effectively silenced the entire vampire population of the episcopal region."

But, it was far from a lasting solution, since the vampire legend remained in force in Greece for more than 100 years. in the History of Roumania, Ureche identified a similar incident of a bishop who fought belief systems: "In 1801, on July 12 The Bishop of Siges makes a request to the governor of Wallachia and asks him to instruct his province's rulers to stop allowing the people of Stroesti must take dead bodies who were already taken away twice on the belief that they were vampires."

This time, it didn't be the case, since as recently even as 1914 N.I. Dumitrascu was writing in Ion Creanga Folklore journal from Romania and a collection of stories from the past:

"Some two or three decades ago, in the commune of Afumati in Dolj in Dolj, an unnamed peasant, Marin Mirea Ociocioc, passed away. It was discovered that his relatives also passed away in succession, one after another. One of them, Badea Vrajitor (Badea the wizard) was able to find him. Badea himself, who was later able to go into the forest, all the way to the frontier during an icy winter night was devoured by the wolves. Bones of Marin had been sprinkled with red wine and a service at the church performed over them, and returned to the grave. After that, there were no other deaths in the family.

"Some fifteen years back around 15 years ago, in Amarasti in northern Dolj an elderly lady mom of the poor Dinu Gheorghita, died. After a while, she's children's oldest son began dying each one by the next then, their children, her son's youngest. The children were frightened, they took her out one night and cut her in two and then laid her to rest again. The deaths would not end. They took her body and buried it another time then what could they discover? The body was completely intact, without wound. It was an amazing sight. They carried her away and took her into the woods, and then placed her beneath the shade of a magnificent tree in a remote section of forest. Then they disemboweled her. extracted her heart where blood was flowing and cut it into four pieces and placed the heart on hot cinders, and then burned it. The ashes were taken they gave to the children to drink water from. They put the body on the flame, then burned it, then buried the remains of the body. Then, the deaths stopped.

"Some 20 or 30 years back, a disabled an unmarried manfrom Cusmir located in the southern part of Mehedinti died. After a short time the death of his relatives, they started to die or fell sick. They complained that their leg was becoming dry. It happened in a variety of places. What's the possibility? Perhaps it's the cripple. Let's get him down. They took him out on Saturday night and discovered him to be as red as red, and wrapped up in the corner in the cemetery. He was cut up and then took the usual measures. They extracted the liver and heart then burned them with red-hot fire, and then distributed the remains to his wife and other relatives who were sick. They consumed them along with water and returned to health.

"In the Cusmir, a different family started to suffer often deaths. Then suspicion began to be centered on an old man who had passed away long ago. When they found him and found him sat in a position reminiscent of an Turk and red as red, as fire, for were he not eating all of a family of young, strong men. When they tried to take him out, he refused with his dirty and disgusting. They hit him with an axeand were able to get him out but were unable to cut him with knives. They used a scythe as well as an axe, and cut out his liver and the heart they burned them, then handed them out to people who were sick to drink. They consumed the drink and recovered their health. The old man was buried and the deaths were put to rest.

"In Vaguilesti, in Mehedinti there was a peasant named Dimitriu Vaideanu, of Transylvanian origin who had married his wife in Vaguilesti and then settled in Mehedinti. His children perished in succession, one after another 7 of them died within a short time after birth, and a few larger ones had passed away too. Many began to question what the root of this might be. They gathered in a council and decided to ride a white horse into the cemetery on a night, to see if it could be able to pass over the graves of relatives of the wife's. They did this and the horse ran over every grave, until it reached the grave of her mother-in-law, Joana Marta, who was a witch who was well-known throughout the world. The horse remained there in the grave, pounding the earth using its heels, neighing and snorting, but unable to get over the grave. There was probably something sinister there. Then, at night, Dimitriu and his son used candles to dig the grave. They were shocked at what they observed. There was a woman in the form of an Turk and with long locks falling across her face, her skin turning red and with nails that were horribly long. They put together brushwood as well as shavings and bits of old crosses. They served wine to her and then put straw in and lit a fire on the entire. They then pushed the earth back , and then went to their homes."

It is interesting to observe that during the battle at Cusmir the body refused to be destroyed. It is one of the rare instances in literature of a vampire trying to stop their body from destruction; most of the instances, the body remains in a state of inactivity, a passive object that is used in the manner that the local peasants would like.

A story about wires that appeared on November 6th, 1902 version of The Brooklyn Daily Eagle, with the headline

"Thought Ghost Stones' Home" offers a fascinating variation on the legend of the vampire "Vienna 6 November A rare story of the superstition that is so common in the peasantry of Hungary is found in the village Gross-Zorlenez close to Reschita. The home of a widow called Pova was recently repeatedly stoned. The police were unable to identify the perpetrator. The son of the widow became obsessed with the notion that his father arose from his grave each night, and bombarded his previous residence and buried his body, visited the cemetery and dug up the body and dragged it for nearly one mile, and then burned the body. The boy was detained."

Similar to this, the Daily Telegraph reported on February 15th 1912 that "A Buda-Pesth, or Budapest message to the Messaggero describes a horrendous instance of superstition. A fourteen-year-old boy died a few weeks ago, in a tiny village. The farmer the work the boy had been and believed his ghost from the deceased was constantly visiting him at night. To end these alleged visits The farmer with several friends, went to the cemetery in the evening, placed three garlic cloves and three stones into the mouth, then inserted the corpse with a stake and secured them to the floor. This was done to free them from the evil spirit as the deceitful farmer and his companions claimed after being detained."

Vampires are generally solitary creatures However, there are reports that vampires hunt in groups. One of them is from a book written by two English writers who lived in Derekuoi the Christian village in Varna, Bulgaria. It was published in 1869. stated:

"At the moment of this incident about five years ago our community was infected by vampires that residents were forced to gather in three or four houses, to light candles throughout the night, and watch each other to stay clear of the attacks of the Obours, who illuminated our streets in their glitter and of which the most inventive cast their shadows over the walls in which the peasants died of fear. Others were screaming, shouting and swore in front of the doors, wandered into abandoned houses and spit blood in the flour, and turned everything upside-down and covered the entire space, including the paintings of saints and the saints, with cow-dung.

"Happily for Derekuoi's mother, an elderly woman suspected of having being a witch discovered the Ilatch [folk medicine] that we previously mentioned, and slayed the troublesome spirits and, since then, the village is free of these unsettling supernatural visits."

The vampire was well-known to the villager population and brought shame on his son. The writers of this book recount the following story: "A servant of ours is the son of a famous vampire. He has been practicing penance in this Lent by not smoking and also not drinking spirits or wine in order to cleanse himself of the mistakes of his father and prevent him from becoming a vampire. . .Poor Theodore is head over ears in the love of Miss Tuturitza The young lady who lives next to him and she is completely in love with his love, however her parents are unable to approve the marriage due to vampire's father."

Photo of an 800-year old skeleton from Bulgaria which was cut in the chest using an iron rod

Although a stake through the heart or chest is the most commonly used method of killing a vampire the diverse and rich folklore offers a myriad of alternatives. For instance, in certain areas of Romania the only thing needed is a needle inserted through the heart. And in another part of the world, people used a spike that was hot red. The body was often treated further like being weighed down by stones or cutting off the head or having the legs taken off and then placed into the shape of an "X" over the chest.

Decapitation is second only one of the methods to stop a heart attack as the best and most common method of stopping the vampire. The head is separated at the base of neck and often in between the legs or even buried only a few inches away to the person. This prevents the body and head from reuniting. In some cases, the body was burnt and the ashes scattered. Or, they could be mixed with water, and served to children in the village to drink. Another more appealing variation of this was to put an unopened bottle of wine close to the grave of the vampire, then uncover it within six weeks, then consume it.

Garlic is commonly used to deter vampires and across Eastern Europe it was common to hang garlic from windows, doors and bedposts in case there was a suspicion that a vampire was operating in the area. Garlic was always displayed at these locations during St. Andrew's Day and St. George's Day, which were considered to be dangerous days for vampire attacks due to reasons that are not fully understood. These dates were considered to be dangerous, and even cows were scrubbed with garlic to prevent vampire from executing them. It was believed that vampires killed livestock, a practice which they shared with witches. All lighting in the house were snuffed out and everyone would wear their shirts inside and out. Also, all equipment and cooking utensils would be turned upside down. This is a typical mythological ward for magic in folklore and the belief that turning things upside-down and then inside out would keep evil from being able to be snuffed out.

There was a belief that garlic was a way to cause the death of a vampire. If the grave was open, instead of putting an iron stake through the heart of the vampire and then putting garlic in the mouth of the vampire. Some believed that stones, millet or nails could perform the same job well.

The notion that strong smells can be able to defeat an animal that is stinky is a popular one. People in Greece who saw bodies exhumed which were treated for vampirism observed that the people would light incense. The reason, according to the villagers did not only reduce the smell of decaying corpses but also to reduce the power of the vampire in the battle to defeat it. In the Philippines the local vampire type known as the Aswang could be defeated by red peppers or a variety of other spices.

In Bulgaria the vampire hunters would hunt down their own local animal known as the Dhampire by filling the bottle with some blood. The hunter would then leave it in a place where Dhampire is able to find it, after which the creature entered the body, turning into in the form of a smoke cloud and then sealed the bottle with the wax, and also an image depicting saints. If the

Dhampire was able to spot the method, the hunter was able to use force to get it inside the bottle by inflicting fear on it by using holy objects. The bottle was later thrown into the fire which melted it, and killed the Dhampire.

Like many other bits of mythology about vampires there are many parallels with other cultures. From the mid-20th century Cajuns as well as African-Americans living in the Deep South hung bottles from the trees that lined their front yards to keep spirits at bay and prevent from entering the home.

Other methods to get rid from the vampire was to set off an open flame over the grave, wrap the coffin with wild roses, tie canes of them to the coffin or put nine distaffs in the grave. The more practical approach was used from the Romanian Gypsies who shot bullets at the grave. If a bullet penetrated the coffin and killed the vampire.

Although garlic is the most commonly used option to fight vampires but there were many other. In Serbia the peasants used the tar to draw an image of a cross on their doors. In Bosnia women, when they went to offer condolences to the family of a person who had passed away in the past, they would put some hawthorns in their headdresses. After leaving they would toss the hawthorn in the trash. The legend was that hawthorn attracted vampires and so those who had passed away would hunt down the small plant, and would not go to their home or follow the home of their neighbors.

Some vampires were invincible to defeat. For instance, the Platnik of Bulgaria was only killed by a bolt lightning (prayers can, of course be invoked to trigger this) or by placing a hot poking through on the weekend. Fortunately, there were many ways to stop the Platnik since it was a timid creature. Wolf skulls, animal skulls, shining light, iron and even fire can scare it away.

It is interesting to note that although vampires and wolves can be found in folklore, the connection has been exaggerated in fictional. Many folklore vampires do not transform into wolves. In fact, many of the vampire legends claim that wolves strike a vampire. The Bulgarian Platnik as well as the Albanian Sampiro and a few others are harassed by the wolves.

A variety of traditions focussed on stopping a person from becoming vampire at all. If someone was at a high risk for becoming a vampire, there was a myriad of ways to prevent the person from becoming a vampire. The most commonly used method of all the traditions to become a vampire however, any sudden and unplanned death, such as drowning or murder was considered suspicious and so were those who had a sinful life or were part of religious minorities, or who were excommunicated. In Russia the belief was that alcoholics had to be vampires, with there was a link between their ruddy appearance in their lives and the ruddy appearance vampires were believed to possess.

The methods varied from place to place and typically involved placing something in the mouth or tied the mouth shut. The object could be different depending on whether it was the form of a rock, a piece from earth, coin or any other variety of other things. The explanation is that it gives the deceased something to chew, as well as preventing the soul from leaving the mouth or letting bad things in the body. This is similar to the reason given for binding the mouth shut, but in some cultures, the tying was believed to be cut prior to burial. Another reason that is more practical could be that the mouth opens and widen when it is dead which gives the body an unsettling appearance that might upset mourners. In Greece the cross was placed over the mouth or the mouth was covered with a piece of pottery bearing an inscription "Christ triumphs!" written on it.

Chapter 4: Wave of Werewolf Attacks

For reasons that aren't fully understood, various tales and myths came together during the Late Middle Ages to form the belief that was prevalent in regions of Europe that people could become wolves at will to hunt animals and humans. They were able to emerge in the unconscious of all people and became legal documents in the 15th century, at exactly the time of the initial waves of witchcraft-related trials. In many instances the defendants were accused being witches and werewolves.

The first major case that took place in Western Europe consisted of a trial in the state of Valais located in what is currently Switzerland which began in 1428. Although this wasn't an initial witch-trial in Europe or even the first trial in Switzerland however, these were the first trials where a significant amount of people were tested and punished for their witchcraft. When the seven years of trial were ended, hundreds were found guilty, and around 200 were executed through burning to death.

It is not clear how the witchcraft hysteria in Valais began and it took place against the midst of political turmoil which led to an revolt against the nobility as well as an attack on the Waldensians which was an ascetic sect of Christianity which was Catholic Church declared to be heretical. The witchcraft craze could be a means to allow the aristocracy and the Church to gain control of the situation, but regardless of the motive there were numerous allegations of individuals against those who were believed as having committed crimes following signing a bargain with Satan. Authorities declared that they would indict or imprison any person who was accused by their acquaintances, and even the nobility was part of the decision. If the accused is pointed to by more than five individuals who were not themselves suspects The accused could be savagely subjected to torture. Then, they'd generally be in court and sentenced to be executed for witchcraft.

In hindsight, it's evident how easily this law could be abused. Anyone with an issue could be able to bring the accusation of witchcraft and those who are sentenced to burn to death could claim their revenge by pointing fingers at the people who sent them to be burned.

Most likely, the entire town was filled with allegations and many of them were of a type that would become well-known in the years to follow. The accusers claimed that witches used spells to hurt livestock and crops as well as cause illness or miscarriages or even cause death. Witches would have meetings in private with the Devil in the form of an animal or a ram or, sometimes, even as schoolmasters who would instruct them on how to commit the wrong thing. Witches would then confess to the good deeds they'd done, and then repent by vowing to do more evil. Witches had created the magical salve which they put on chairs to enable them to glide through the air.

A tiny portion of the trials alleged that people were who werewolves and had gotten authority from the Devil to slaughter livestock. The connection between werewolves and witches would persist throughout the witch-hunting craze. one of the numerous crimes that were in alliance with the Devil were believed to have committed.

In contrast to the later witch trials, around two-thirds of those suspects were witches and werewolves, and the majority are males. The trend was not just in Switzerland as well, but all over the witch-hunting craze, and the connection to witches as well as werewolves was mostly viewed as a male-dominated one. Witches who were female were not often thought of as wolves.

A male werewolf-witch took place within Arnhem, Netherlands in 1595 In 1595, Johan Martensen von Steenhuisen was accused of being a werewolf. He was first subjected to dunking, which is a method to detect witches, in which people are bound and thrown into the water. If they sink then the person is innocent. If they're witches, the water is against them and they are able to float.

Martensen floated and admitted to selling his heart in the hands of Martensen, who was floating in the water. He confessed to selling his Devil three years prior. He was walking along the dyke after suffering an injury and was feeling depressed when he met an unknown person. He requested the stranger to bring him some food. At that point, Martensen's friend said that

Martensen could eat anything the he likes, and more if he left God.

With some hesitation, Martensen decided to agree to the deal, and the Devil handed him an item of cloth saying that for as long as it was there and was able to use it, he would be successful in anything the work he set his mind to. At that time it was "walking like an Wolf." What he needed to do was place the cloth over his head to change. He was able to retain the mental faculties of a human, but the only thing he could do was speak. He also could employ the cloth to trick people to hit them with the cloth.

Jose Luiz Bernardes Ribeiro's photo of a dunking crane taken from Germany

66

After the concept of werewolves was ingrained on the minds of people everywhere and it didn't take long before individuals were tried for being shapeshifters with no accusations of witchcraft.

Certain depraved people committed crimes so terrible that the general public believed that they were werewolves since no human being could ever have committed such horrific crimes. One example is Gilles Garnier, a 16th century hermit from France who was a resident of Dole, the city of Dole. Despite his isolation and inability to earn a living the man he was with found his wife. After a while, any marital bliss that could have been in the secluded hut was broken when he was unable to not support her. She began complaining, and Garnier was desperate.

In the month of October 1572 the first victim he assaulted was in 1572, a girl aged 10 who was a victim of his own and then took to a vineyard out of town. Then he smothered the girl to death, stripped her and took huge bites out of her thighs and arms. In the end, thinking of his annoying wife who was at home He cut off a small portion of the girl's body and brought it back to cook it for her.

After a couple of weeks, he assaulted his second victim, also a girl of a younger age, whom was jumped on and began to bite and slash at however, a number of people rushed to the shouts of the girl and he ran to flee. The girl was severely injured and passed away a few days after.

The next year, Garnier struck again, this time killing a 10-year-old boy , eating his flesh from his belly and thighs as well as taking one of his legs with him home. Then , he strangled another to death but was discovered and was forced to flee before he could consume the corpse.

The second attack, this time on a boy in his early teens that was more brutal. The boy was killed and ate so much the stomach of the child that he literally cut the child's body in two.

All of these assaults occurred in 1572. The next year, he smothered an innocent girl and then in the recognizable manner, ate her flesh right there and brought some with him to take home for his wife.

The residents believed that there was a werewolf roaming around the area, so the authorities issued an order allowing ordinary citizens to hunt down and kill the creature should they be able to. At first they were unable to locate the monster that was believed to be in the area, but at night, a group of workers from the town nearby were walking in the evening when they saw what they believed to be an animal with a baby in its mouth. They then realized that one of them was Gilles Garnier. They alerted authorities and the man was taken into custody.

Garnier was beaten up however, he didn't appear to require much support to confess to his crimes. Maybe it was because of the amount of evidence that was thrown at Garnier, or perhaps his own perception that he appeared mentally unstable. He claimed that he'd been out hunting in the woods at night, and was confronted by a ghost who gave him the key to a particular ointment which transformed you into an wolf which made it much easier for him to hunt. He confessed to all charges and was accused of lycanthropy as well as witchcraft. The latter was because of his agreement with the specter whom the court determined to have been an agent for the Devil.

Over 50 witnesses admitted that they witnessed the man slashing children. This is why one has to wonder why he wasn't detained earlier. A lot of witnesses believed they saw the wolf. The majority of the time, the incident occurred in the evening and Garnier's shaggy clothing, rough appearance, and wild behavior made many people believe that they saw an animal , rather than a human. It's also possible witnesses didn't see anything, but instead held a hatred for Garnier and wanted to be sure that he was found guilty.

Gilles Garnier was sentenced to death and burned to death on the 18th of January 1573. His wife was detained and burnt the following day. While under torture, she confessed to aiding him and eating foods that were forbidden. She was not suspected as a Werewolf However, her deeds were thought to be a crime of such a nature that it would be punished the same way.

In the past, looking back on the incident, it is clear to us that Garnier was an infamous serial murderer. The eyes of the 16th century rural Frenchmen However Garnier had to be more than actually a creature disguised as a human.

Another man like this is Peter Stubbe, a prosperous farmer who lived in Bedburg located in Rhineland within what was called the Holy Roman Empire. Stubbe (also identified in different documents in various sources as Stuppe, Stumpp, or Stumpf) was enduring difficult times. The region had been devastated by the Cologne War, a bitter conflict among Protestants and Catholics which historians have interpreted as a precursor towards the Thirty Years War, the most violent religious conflict Europe has ever witnessed. The region was under the control of the Catholics however Stubbe was a Protestant who did not want to convert. That could be a reason to make him an easy target.

In the late 1580s, people and animals from the area were found dead and their bodies ripped in horrifying ways. Many believed that a wolf of enormous size was to blame and spoke of it in exaggerated language "with eyes large and big that in the dark shimmered like flames, with an enormous mouth and wide with sharp and brutal

teeth, a large body and powerful claws."
This beast is surely not an ordinary one,
but rather waswolf.

For a long time the wolf had a hard time
escaping capture. Many hunters pursued it
, but to no avail until 1589 when the
hunters along with their dogs finally drove
down the wolf. In the brush they pursued
the vicious beast, and eventually managed
to surround it. The cordon was tightened
but were surprised to discover they had
not caught a wolf, instead, Peter Stubbe.

But the hunters didn't fall for it. In the
previous encounter, someone succeeded in
cutting off the left forepaw of the wolf as
well Stubbe had lost his hand. This was all
the evidence they required. The hunter
was brought before the magistrate who
ordered him to go on the stand, and He
quickly confessed, preferring not to be
tortured. Stubbe confessed that he
murdered thirteen children as well as two
pregnancies women, and one man. After
killing the women who were pregnant then
he cut the babies out of their wombs, and
then consumed their hearts.

According to a pamphlet released soon
after his trial Stubbe declared:

"Peeter was a man who, from his youth was extremely prone to sin and the practice of evil arts at the age of twelve up to twenty years of age, and onwards until his death and acquainting himself with the dreadful desire for necromancy, magic and sorcery, he acquaints himself with many evil creatures and spirits, so that he was unable to remember the God who created him and the Savior who sacrificed his blood for mankind's redemption. At the end, a lack of care of salvation entrusted both body and soul to the Devil forever, in exchange for a the pleasure of a small amount in this world, so in order to be famous and be praised in the world, even though the heavens were lost to him.

"The Devil, who hath an ear that is always open to the sexually sexy whims of men cursed, promised to grant him whatever desires his heart had in his lifetime. the vile wretch never desired the riches or promotions and was not fulfilled by any pleasure that was external or outside however, he had a tyrannical heart and a brutal bloody mind, he asked that at his whim it could work his malice on women, men, and even children, as a animal, so that he could remain in peace, without fear or risk of death, and be unable to be the one who executed any bloody undertaking was his intention to commit.

"The Devil, who saw him as a perfect instrument for mischief, as a wicked fend, enthralled by the desire for wrong and destruction, offered him a girdle, which after being put on and he was transformed into the appearance of a hungry devouring wolf, powerful and powerful with eyes that were large and big, that at night, sparkled flames of fire. with a mouth that was large and broad with sharp and brutal teeth, a massive body and powerful feet. He was not even able to take off the same girdle than now he would be in the same form as he was before in accordance with the proportions of the man and appear as if he'd never been altered.

" ..." he was able to carry out various heinous and horrible murders. If any person was dissatisfied with him, he'd seek revenge, and at no time did they or any of them leave the fields or around the city however, in the form of a wolf, he'd soon meet them, and never stop until the time he was able to slit their throats, and torn their joints to pieces. After he'd had an experience of this that he was so enthralled and joy in the shedding of blood that he would all night and day, walk through the fields and engage in extreme brutalities. In the evenings, when he walked those streets in Collin, Bedbur, and Cperadt with a smile, and in a manner that was a bit comical and in a manner that was very civil, being well-known by all who resided there and was often received a standing ovation from those whose acquaintances and children he slaughtered although no one was suspected of the similar. In these areas I'm saying the man would go between the streets and if he was able to see a woman, maid or child whom his eyes adored or his heart desired then he would wait for to see them leave the town or city. If he were able to at all find them by themselves or on the field slash the animals, and then after with his wolfish semblance, he would brutally kill them."

The lusts of his were even extended to his family members: "He had at that time a beautiful young damsel with his daughter. After whom was also infatuated and brutally commit the an incestuous and sexy affair together." Also, he killed his son in wolf form , and then consumed his brains.

After having heard all this, the stunned judge sentenced Stubbe to execution in a gruelling sentence "their various judgments were pronounced on the 28th of October 1589 in this manner, which is to say that Stubbe Peeter, who was the main criminal, was first judged to be placed on a wheel and to be slashed with red hot pincers placed in ten places , to have his flesh extracted from the bones. Following that the arms and legs to be smashed with the use of a hatchet or a wood ax followed by having his head smashed off his bodyand then to be burned to an ash. His daughter and gossip (wife) were found to be slain quickly to ashes, at the same day and at the same time as the body of the said Stubbe Peeter. On the 31st day of the same month they died at the foot in Bedbur with the assistance of several nobles and princes from Germany."

Was Stubbe an alleged serial killer or was he just a scared individual who would inform the judges whatever that they would like to be told to keep from being tortured? It's difficult to be certain. He must have realized that, even if he avoided discomfort during the interrogation process and apologizing for his crimes could cause much more suffering later on and even the possibility of death. Giles Garnier had been caught in the act, however there was no massive evidence against Peter Stubbe. It is also interesting that the involvement of daughter and wife is a further layer of mystery, and particularly because the sources don't know the circumstances in which they were involved in the murders. From the things Stubbe admitted to doing with his child, the two might have been victims of abuse who were caught in the mass hysteria, instead of being the perpetrators.

The most obvious example of the serial killer being labelled waswolf is the case of Manuel Blanco Romasanta, one of the most recent werewolf trials to date.

Romasanta is believed to be intersex. When he was born in 1809 the midwife or doctor who delivered him was said to be to be a girl. He was raised in that manner for the next six years, until an obstetrician noticed the mistake and told his parents that they were expecting a boy.

Despite his rough start He appeared superficially to be a well-integrated. He was able the art of writing and reading in a time that was not commonplace in the working class. He also was a tailor and was married. After his wife's death at the age of 1833, his father turned an agent for sales, and traveled across Spain as well as Portugal. It was not known that he was using his trips to conceal a number of murderous crimes.

It is not known the number of people killed by Romasanta but the first confirmed instance was that of a constable from Leon in Spain who, in 1844, attempted to collect a due of 600 Reales Romasanta owed to a dealer for the products that he was selling. The constable was found dead , and Romasanta was missing. He was in absentia found guilty as well as sentenced to 20 years prison.

He left for Portugal in the course of a year , he was in a small village, working various jobs , and helping in the harvest. A lot of the males in the village considered him to be asexual due to his small size, slim stature, informal, non-sexual relations with different women and also the fact that he spun yarn on a wheel.

Because of his in-depth understanding of the country due to his experience as a salesman on the road Many people hired him as a guide. He would often take advantage of the opportunity to take them to a remote location and then kill them. He was a trusted guide and would often accompany lone women, or mothers with children, who were his preferred victims. The bodies, once found were horribly mutilated and looked like they had been ripped apart by a predator large enough to take them. Initially it was possible to avoid suspicion by writing letters to the families of his victims, stating they were safe. The suspects probably induced the victims to write these letters prior to their murder and promised to take them away "when they reached the scene."

Although he succeeded in accumulating a huge list of his victims' names, he did make the mistake of selling the clothes of his victims. In the time of his victims, the majority of people had the same clothes on every day, meaning that the clothes could be easily identified and people started to pay attention. They also pondered the brand new soap Romasanta was selling, and speculation was circulating that it was created by consuming the fat of victims he killed.

He was detained, charged with murder, and swiftly confessed. He claimed that he killed 13 people in the course of suffering from the disease of Lycanthropy. Judges scoffed and challenged him to change into the form of a wolf before the court. To which the wolf gave a somewhat inconvenient reply that he had no anymore a werewolf.

The judge found that he was guilty of nine murders, and ruled that the remaining four victims were actually murdered by wolves. In the beginning, they sent him to the death penalty however, an French doctor demanded the stay of execution to ensure that it could be able to study Romasanta who, he believed, was suffering from severe delusions. The field of psychology was still in its early stages at the period, and this bizarre case was bound to provoke a furore within healthcare institutions. The plea to pardon him from his final punishment was pushed all the way to the Queen Isabel II. The request was granted and Romasanta passed away from stomach cancer on 1863. still being held in prison for his numerous infractions.

A sketch from the present of Romasanta in
an medical report

Chapter 5: A Holy Werewolf

A case that isn't within the general framework is the case of Thiess of Kaltenbrun who confessed to being was a werewolf on 1692 in Jurgensburg, Swedish Livonia, which is today Zaube, the capital city. Zaube within Latvia. At the time, Thiess was in her 80s and probably not fully control of his mind. He appeared in the court to testify in an investigation into the man who was accused of robbing the church. As he stood on the witness stand however, instead of discussing the matter, he began to talk about his status as an obedient werewolf.

Thiess claimed that he and unknown friends were granted the ability to lycanthropize by God to turn into wolves to fight evil spirits in Hell. They would visit three times per all through the year "during the evening of Pentecost and during Midsummer's Night, and on Saint Lucia's Night. Concerning those two first nights of the year were concerned, they didn't go in the exact manner on those nights and more so when the crop was flowering. This because it is when the seeds begin to sprout that the sorcerers take the blessing and send it to Hell then it is at this point that the werewolves decide in order to get it to bring it back out again."

So, he and his colleagues "hounds from God" were basically the holy raiding party that was created to recover stolen items by witches. There were many witch trials that included accusations that witches employed their power to take advantage of their neighbors, however, the accusers didn't explain why defendants were generally not better off than the claimed victims. Thiess resolved this issue by explaining that witches took all their riches to Hell.

He said he owned an exclusive belt made out of a werewolf's pelt, which was used to transform him into a wolf. The belt was gifted to him by an agriculturalist. This is a classic tale that is a part of Germanic as well as Scandinavian folklore that is found in a variety of stories. Thiess claimed that he had given away the belt the previous 10 years. The court asked the names of two individuals, at which the point Thiess changed his mind and stated the belt was not there and all they needed to do was go to the bush, strip the bushes, and then they would transform into werewolves.

He also told a myriad of bizarre stories, the majority of which had to amend after his inquisitors found his story in contradiction or demanded more information. He altered his version of how he came to be werewolves and again, this time telling the story of how a werewolf had toasted him and granted him the ability. Thiess claimed that all he had to do to transfer lycanthropy was toast someone using a jug of alcohol, breathe in the booze three times, and say, "You will become like me." Then in the event that the person consumed from the bottle, he was transformed into werewolves. At this point, no one was willing to participate.

He also claimed of the fact that last year's great harvest was due to him for having conducted a successful raid into Hell. The judges also noted that he claimed to not be a werewolf for 10 years, and at that the judge questioned him. Thiess admitted to lying about this and was an werewolf.

Some of his assertions were confirmed by his reputation in the community. Many of his neighbors had long ruminated that werewolves were involved with the Devil like all werewolves were believed to be. There is no doubt that the old man was recounting his tales on various occasions however, many did not believe in these claims. Indeed, many thought him a good citizen and nobody thought he was crazy.

The judge now needed to determine the best way to deal with the man and his bizarre tale. What Thiess admitted to was a crime that is considered capital however, his confession was so ambiguous that they could not really be able to convict him? To clarify the situation and possibly to offer an elderly man with no resources an opportunity to escape They asked him whether he was a genuine Lutheran who was a regular attender and regularly attended church. Thiess stated that he did not perform any of the usual actions of worship because he couldn't know what they were.

The judges were not convinced that the werewolf was real, however they did apologize for witchcraft. Many of the locals claimed that the werewolf was a practitioner of traditional magic and folklore, blessing horses or healing wounded. He was a magician with a charm that he would intone to certain spells. They were "Sun and moon travel over the sea, bring back the soul the Devil took to Hell and grant the animals health and life that was stolen from them."

The judges declared this it was a clear instance of witchcraft since Thiess never mentioned God in her charm. At the end of the day, they sent him to prison and banished, which is a gentle sentence given that most condemned witches were burned or hanged on the stake.

Chapter 6: Mistaken Identities

Prior to being hunted to close to death in the 19th century there were wolves in the rural regions of Europe however, generally speaking the population had nothing to fear as wolves did not often assaulted humans. However, they do attack livestock however, and thus were considered to be a nuisance. occasionally in winter, particularly where wolves had no other food source There were cases of travelers who were victimized by wolves and even big packs making their way into the areas of occupation to hunt for human flesh. In most cases, the killers were believed to be werewolves.

One of them was the Werewolf of Ansbach The wolf was a scourge of in the Principality of Ansbach during Ansbach in the Holy Roman Empire in 1685. The wolf initially began attacking livestock, but eventually it became more aggressive and began to eat children. As it did it was believed by the locals that they were witnessing the reincarnation of the recently dead Burgermeister who was a brutal man whose funeral was so dreadful that nobody shed tears. The Burgermeister returned as a werewolf, they said and then decided to take it down.

A group of hunters with their dogs were able to pull the animal out of the forest and protect it from the elements and at that point, the wolf jumped into a ditch. The hunters killed the animal and took it back to town in which it was able to have its muzzle removed and put on man's outfit, which included a mask, wig, and fake beard to look as the famous Burgermeister.

A more recent and bloodier incident was Gevaudan, the Beast of Gevaudan. The attacks took place in the remote region in southern France in 1764. the wolf was large and had an unusual, reddish-colored pelt was a threat to the countryside. The primary victim was shepherd girl known as Janne Boulet. It then began to target other peasants who were lone mostly children and women. There were some who were to be mutilated beyond recognition, while others vanished completely. Shepherds soon became afraid of tending their flocks and one would want to enter the rural region alone. Guard dogs did not aid since they were prone to escape whenever the beast was seen.

In the month of October the beast grew bolder and even moved into a village during daylight which is not something that wolves often do. Jean-Pierre Pourcher was working in his barn in Julianges when a shadow snuffed out the afternoon sun through the window. He was able to see the furious face of the Wolf. Frightened, Pourcher grabbed his shotgun and empty both barrels of it. Although he struck both times the beast didn't end up dying. Instead, it cried out in pain , and then ran away appearing to be no less swollen.

The body count increased from a few to hundreds, before reaching 100. Local hunters were unable capture the beast, which showed a shrewdness that matched its appetite. The government decided to take action and offer a substantial reward, and sending many soldiers as well as volunteers on hunts organized by the government. Soldiers even dressed up as women for the purpose of attracting the beast.

The details of the attacks were widely circulated throughout France and were spread through the rather new medium of newspapers. The bizarre and terrifying descriptions of the creature and the brutality of the assaults on children and women, that saw them decapitated and disemboweled, created a smoky excitement for those who read. It also showed the French that despite their rich cultural esteem, their extensive global empire and rapid growth of literacy, there was still mystery in the more remote parts of their country.

All told it was estimated that the Beast of Gevaudan attacked some 300 people, but the majority of them were not killed. The day's newspapers interviewed survivors, and their testimony contributed to the blood-curdling character of the tale.

Some of them even were minor stars. When a group of kids working with cattle was attacked on the 12th of January 1765, a twelve-year-old young man named Jacques portefaix gathered his friends and attempted to stop the beast using pikes. They struck the beast with their primitive weapons, which were simple sticks with simple iron points. The wolf was able to capture an 8-year-old boy. However, the other animals stabbed at it until they let the boy go. The beast then grabbed a second boy, and the other animals needed to come to their aid. The wolf carried the boy to a slough. children surrounded it and stabbed it multiple times. The wolf threw its prey away and then fought back and was then stabbed many times. After being repeatedly pricked and having twice lost its meal the wolf ran away. Both boys suffered serious injuries but both survived. The king Louis XV was so impressed that he paid a substantial sum to each and also educated youngsters Jacques on his own cost. He was later promoted to an artillery lieutenant and was promoted to a higher position than he would have thought of if he was an unknown peasant.

On the 11th of August 1765 the beast swarmed Marie-Jeanne Valet who was a young girl who managed to defeat the giant beast and even injure it. She was on the farm of a nearby family and was heading home, on her own, when she heard noises in the distance, swung her head, and was confronted by the jaws of slavery of The Beast of Gevaudan.

The beast had taken her by the banks of a river. Marie-Jeanne was ready. She carried an unprepared spear as all was doing in the terrifying moment. She dropped it into the chest of the wolf after which it let loose a scream and then put its paw on the wound, making an oddly human gesture, then fell to the bottom of the river. The girl fled back to her house and was unable to see what transpired to the wolf at that time however, it was evident that it escaped the wound and continued to hunt Marie-Jeanne's friends. Marie-Jeanne was celebrated as the noble "Maiden of Gevaudan," defending her body from the hungry demands of wild animals. A monument in her honor remains in the Auvers village of Auvers close to the spot where she stood.

The wolf's distinctive reddish fur has been noticed before. Numerous other odd information was circulated regarding its appearance, which led to the issue of whether it was even a wolf. Many speculated that it was an escapee beast or another creature from prehistoric times. The eyewitnesses, their vision probably distorted due to the terror of facing the beast, said it was the size of the size of a horse, and had long hair that was shaggy and an snout that resembled the calf. Many claimed the hind legs of the creature ended in hooves instead of the paws. It was able to make leaps of great length and even sit on its hind legs and was immune to shooting. Many claimed they could talk French and walk through water. Many even claimed that it had been killed numerous times, and was able to come back to life from its grave.

It certainly did be repeatedly stabbed and shot and returned to take additional victims. Traps were used to escape and poisonous bait was left on the table was ate with no harm. Every time hunter groups went out back empty handed. Dissatisfied with the slow progress, Louis XV was furious. Louis XV eventually sent his personal bodyguard and gun-bearer, Francois Antoine, along with a group of hunters who were experienced. In 1765, in September, the king declared his victory, proudly displaying the body of a large wolf that he shot. It was 100 pounds in weight and about six feet long. Antoine was able to return to Versailles and took the prize the king had promised, and he was the toast in French society. He was given the title of "grand-croix from the Order of Saint-Louis" and was granted a salary of 1,000 pounds. His son, who been with him during hunting trips, was promoted to an officer in a cavalry organization and his family earned an excellent income by displaying the animal stuffed in stylish Parisian drawing rooms and at country fairs.

It turned out this wasn't the end the story. In just two years, attacks been rekindled. The beast was responsible for the deaths of at least thirty more people over the following 18 months. Requests to the palace were not heard, if it was because no one from the court was willing to talk to the king about the issue. In the end, however, it was clear that Beast of Gevaudan was dead by the king, as he had ordered that, and to challenge the king would be asking questions about the king.

Again, the inhabitants of Gevaudan attempted to kill this animal but to no avail until a local hunter known as Jean Chastel set out alone. According to his story that he had made a silver amulet, which he used to make bullets. set off to a mountainous region where the beast was observed several times and then sat down to study the Bible. He thought that by seeing one person alone the beast would be drawn to him.

The gun did indeed fire that, and Chastel took his musket and took aim and fired it to death. The date was June 19, 1767. The terror reign was gone.

It is fascinating that silver was used in the making of the bullet. Silver bullets are uncommon in the literature of werewolves, before the idea was taken by novelists in the 18th century. In this instance it's unclear if the bullet's effectiveness was due to the fact that it was made of an object of worship or simply because it was made from silver, or both.

Unfortunately, this animal was not kept. Chastel killed it during the summer heat and it began to decay. It was then opened but one shoulder from a small girl was found in the stomach. Chastel wasn't recognized by the king, and only received a small amount of money from the local authorities however, they did believe the story. The nation's government mocked him and called him as a fraud. In the Gevaudan region Gevaudan however the region was a place where he was the hero of the region. His legacy is still cherished to this day with books, statues, poems and even movies on his adventures.

Modern scholars believe that there were actually a number of Beasts of

Gevaudan. For one thing they both Francois Antoine and Jean Chastel returned with dead wolves. Other hunters claimed victory as well. One hunter snared a wolf which weighed 130 pounds, more than double the weight of a typical wolf. The wolves Antoine and Chastel exhibited to the King were also very large. Maybe there was a group of hungry, oversized animals that were roaming around the fields and forests around Gevaudan.

It is certainly stretching the credibility of thinking that just one animal is responsible for all of the attacks. Of the 240 incidents recorded (and there could have been more) the beasts (or beasts) killed 112 victims and injured 53 others. It's not known the number of farm animals consumed, but there is an overwhelming likelihood that the figure is higher than human deaths toll.

A painting by an artist of The Beast of Gevaudan

Although Gevaudan's Beast (or Beasts) of Gevaudan was the most horrific man killer ever recorded however it wasn't an exclusive case. In all of Europe there are evidence from the medieval and the early modern era of wolf attacks that killed people. They were usually caused only by lone animals who attacked wanderers or shepherds, but often entire packs or multiple victims were at risk.

The most famous case was in Paris during the winter of 1450 in Paris. It was a particularly cold one and there was not much for the wolves to eat in the forest outside of the city to eat , so in the evening, they would sneak into the city. Paris at the time was a city with walls, but the walls were built two centuries earlier and were in disrepair, with many gaps through which animals could pass through. Then, people began to be assaulted right in the center of the city, a unexpected and disturbing event. Although medieval cities weren't the most desirable cities to live in due to crime, contagion and raw sewage being the daily things of daily life, people believed they were protected away from animals that roamed the wild.

Around 40 Parisians were slaughtered, prior to a massive hunt being conducted to kill the group. The hunters stood by until the pack reached the heart of the city at night and then sealed off the streets. After they had the wolves inside the dragnet, they started to tighten it with bows and spears, to lead the animals towards the Ile de la Cite in the city's center. Then, they attacked them and killed in the square right facing Notre Dame.

The Wolf pack of Paris weren't believed to possess supernatural powers, like that of Beast of Gevaudan or some other man killers However, often these animals were believed to be more than what they appeared to be. The notion of eating wolves by man being more than mere hungry predators was officially recognized in the infamous witch hunt book Malleus Maleficarum, first printed in 1487. The author wrote extensively on witches, but also granted a tiny amount of space for the wolf. The book stated:

"What should we think of Wolves that may seize and eat Men and Children from their cradles If this is caused by Witches.

"There is a nagging question regarding wolves. They occasionally snatch people and children out of their homes, consume them, and then move about with such adroitness that with no ability or strength, they can be injured or caught. It's true that this may be due to the natural cause however, it is also due to a glamor, caused by witches. As for the first cause, Blessed Albertus from his classic book On Animals says that it could be triggered by five different causes. Sometimes due to great hunger, when stags or other beasts have come closer to human beings. Sometimes, it is due to the strength of their ferocity like in cases of dog breeds living in the cold regions. But that's not the point. We believe that these things result from an illusion by the devils, as God is punishing a nation for their sins. Check out Leviticus xxvi: If you don't obey my commands I will send creatures of the field to you and will devour your livestock and you. Also, Deuteronomy xxxii Also, I will unleash the beast's teeth on them, etc.

"As to the issue of whether they are real wolves or devils that appear in this form, we believe that they are real wolves, but they are controlled by demons, and get enthralled in two different ways. This could happen without the intervention of witches. And so it was the case of two forty boys who were eaten by two bears who came from the woods because they mocked Elisaus the prophet by saying, "Go up, thou headless and so on. In the same way, it was the lion who killed the prophet who did not follow the commands from God (III. Kings xiii). It is also reported that a bishop from Vienna required the minor litanies to be chanted solemnly on specific days prior to The Feast of the Ascension, since wolves were infiltrating the city and consuming people.

"But in a different way, it could be a trick performed by witches. Because William of Paris describes a person who believed that he was transformed into a wolf and at certain times , he went to hide in caves. Because he was there at a specific time and did not leave the cave for long, still, he believed it was a wolf who was eating children even though the Devil was possessed by the form of a wolf, was actually performing this act, the man

100

mistakenly believed that he was running in the night. He was the entire time disoriented that he finally found in the wood , raving. The Devil enjoys such actions and has created the illusion of pagans believing that humans and women aged over were transformed into beasts. This reveals that such events only occur through the permission of God in conjunction with the devil's work, and not because of any natural flaw; because there is no way or skill could wolves get injured or caught. In this connection, Vincent of Beauvais (in Spec. Hist. VI, 40) says that in Gaul in the time before the Incarnation of Christ and prior to the Punic War, a wolf was able to take a sentry's weapon out the sheath."

The Dr. Johann Geiler von Kaysersberg was a pastor in Strasbourg was a preacher in Strasbourg. He gave an address in 1508 on werewolves. He dismissed the notion of shapeshifters, and stating that the majority of the attacks were hungry wolves who could not locate any other source of food or animals that are unusually aggressive have a craving for human flesh, turn into the usual man-killers. In some cases the author conceded that it could have been the result of "the Devil, who transforms himself and gives his form as the Wolf. So writes Vincentius in his Speculum Historiale. He has adapted it from Valerius Maximus from his time during the Punic War. When the Romans engaged in battle against the people from Africa and the captain was asleep, there was a wolf that pulled out his sword and then carried it away. This was the Devil in the form of a wolf. It's like William of Paris: an animal can kill and devour children and cause the most ill-fated perfidy. One man believed that he was actually one of the wolves. Afterward, he was discovered in the woods, and he died of pure hunger."

Chapter 7: Vampires Beyond Europe

An illustration of an Manananggal in Filipino folklore

The notion the evil creature sucking vitality out the bodies of victims are universal, but a close analysis of a variety of these myths shows that they are not necessarily vampires since they don't conform to the basic Eastern European definition of a dead person returning to life in order to feed the living. The spreading of European ideas via colonialism and later , mass media, has created iconic European myths about vampires across many areas, however some vampires are native to the region in which they reside and are typically blood-sucking ghosts or demons.

Immigration introduced Old World beliefs to the New World, and there are numerous reports regarding vampires found in American newspaper articles from between the 18th and 19th century. The Norwich Evening Courier from Connecticut reported on the 20th of May 1854, that a man called Henry Ray had contracted consumption (tuberculosis) and passed away. The two of his children, both young and healthy, suffered from the disease and passed away. The third son was also diagnosed with the disease, the entire family went to the cemetery and buried the two brothers and then burned their bodies. There was a reason why the father who was the last to die, wasn't exhumed. The reason why this was not done isn't clear. The three sons, and the third received an exorcism with the hope to get rid of the disease. The same thing didn't work and he died in 1854. The press deemed the whole incident to be an example that showed "unreasoning ignorantness and blind belief."

It is also worth noting that the West Indies were also not in the least. The West Indies were not immune. Trinidad There is also the Sukuyan who appears as either a young woman or man and is able to walk around during the the daytime. It's unusual in folklore that it requires permission to enter a home and is largely the work of fiction writers. It'll knock at the door and ask to borrow an item of a small size If permission is granted, it will return at night to slowly draw blood from the victim over the course of several nights. It is the only method to safeguard your home is to chant, "Thursday, Friday, Saturday Sunday" three times, while performing the sign of crossing each opening and every window. If the Sukuyan returns it will escape to the next ward and change into a animal. The person who is bitten must catch the animal and then stone it to death or burn it alive.

In India women are dead when they die during birth or suffer an unnatural death , such as murder. If it happens during the celebration of Diwali the dead will be brought back as a particularly nasty type of revenant referred to as Churel. Churel. With unwashed hair and a tongue that is black, and feet with a backwards sloping They can transform into a beautiful , young woman, in order to charm male relatives of theirs before they drain out their blood, one at a time and transform to old-fashioned men. The Churel is then able to turn to other men and turn into an unwelcome threat to the entire neighborhood.

In Japan in Japan, the Gaki represents the soul of the greedy who returns as a pale-skinned man with a massive stomach filled with blood even though it does not appear to be sucking blood. The mere fact of its existence can be enough to drain its victims, however other varieties of Gaki are known to consume souls, flesh or the thoughts of someone contemplating, or even the topknots of the samurai. Similar to many vampire beliefs Gaki is one of them. Gaki can change it into various forms such as a mist, animals, human like devil with red skin and horns or even specific individuals.

A portrait of Gakis

An additional Japanese vampire to be found is Shuten Doji, an ugly revenant sporting claws that are long. Though it's ugly and deformed it can be awe-inspiring using its flute. is used to induce its victims in a state of state of trance. Then, it will cut the person in the music by its claws, and then consume the blood of their victim.

They Inuit have a bizarre vampirism mythology that is especially suited to their climate. It is believed that the Aipalookvik is the decomposing body of a drowning body that is brought to the shore to take in the living and take the body heat. The creature is created due to an unholy spirit that possesses the body, and this spirit takes over the person's memories and personality.

Many cultures that are not Western, such as the ancient ones like the ones from Babylon and Assyria are awash with stories of evil spirits that reside in the dead. These are what today would be referred to as cases of demonic possession , instead of actual vampires.

Latin America strays even further away from European tradition. Its Mexican

Chupacabra ("goat sucker") is a tiny humanoid that has experienced numerous changes over the course of. The first recorded account dates from 1540 and describes them to be tiny men with dark scales. They each carried a torch and a spear, and were able to attack in large numbers. Since then Chupacabras have been described in many different ways. Chupacabra is described various ways based on the fashions of the time. Today the Chupacabra appears like an alien of gray, with fins at the rear of its head and spine. According to their name they draw blood of goats and other animals.

A representation of an Chupacabra

Otherwhere in Latin America, especially Brazil There's the Chupa-Chupa ("suck sucking") an intense bright red light that is emitted from the sky, and strikes the victim on the chest. The light burns the victim's body and spits out the blood in a huge amount which leaves the victim in a state of weakness in the stomach, feverish, and with an unending headache. It's therefore possible to imagine the legends of UFOs and vampires merging. In fact, contemporary theories on the Chupacabra claim it's some kind of escapee pet of The Gray Aliens.

In the Philippines In the Philippines, the Aswang is a mythological vampire that is believed to exist even today. Since the country is comprised of over 7,000 islands, and nearly as many different local traditions, it's no surprise that tales about the Aswang differ widely. In general, it's thought to represent a female that can transform into a huge animal or pig and then sucks blood out of the victims. It is a favorite of pregnant women (from which it suckers the foetus).

Africa is also home to vampiric monsters and spirits, and a recent report suggests the existence of more popular vampires. The BBC published on December 23 2002 in a report titled "'Vampires attack

Malawi villages" in which it was reported that the southern region of Malawi was under the grips of a vampire panic. Many individuals claimed to have been victimized, with one reporting a scratch in her arm, wherein a vampire had inserted needles to drain blood. Strangers were targeted for the fear of being the blood thieves and one person was even smuggled to death. The fear was underpinned by the spectre of xenophobic and antigovernment hysteria and people claimed that the government was working with blood thieves for international aid organizations to obtain food aid.

Then, in West Africa, people talk about the Isithfuntela, a revenant made by a witch using the body of someone who took their own life. The witch sifts through from the dead body and cuts away the tongue, then inserts a wooden peg into the head. The body then becomes an ancestor of the dead and completely bound to its creator. It needs blood to survive , and it can raise entire legions of the dead to help it in its quest, but only in the nighttime. Although it is physically weak, the Isithfuntela is physically insignificant it can be hypnotized by the victims of its plight and put a wooden rod through their brains so that it can consume blood at will. It can be killed with the standard methods of placing a stake into the heart or by decapitation however sometimes this was not needed because wolves dislike the Isithfuntela and can cut it down whenever they see one.

Chapter 8: Vampires in Popular Culture

19th century lithograph depicting men who

are trying to destroy the vampire

A vampire is depicted in Max Ernst's Une Semaine de Bonte

At the turn of 19th-century, pop fiction was enjoying a boom. Printing at a low cost coupled with the rise of reading and leisure time led to an enormous market for novels. They were usually serialized in low-cost pamphlets, which were released weekly. In fact some of the greatest writers of the period like Charles Dickens had their novels serialized in this manner.

Although there were vampires in popular literature for a long time, the very first bestseller for the genre is The Vampyre by John Polidori published in 1819. The vampire Lord Ruthven is a charming but brutal aristocrat that literary scholars believe was inspired by Lord Byron. Lord Ruthven is a blood-based vampire however he doesn't possess one of the characteristics typical of folklore's vampires for instance, being buried in his grave and being affected by the garlic. He is fond of taking food from beautiful young women, which contributed to the story's appeal by adding an element of sexual innuendo, which is common in the literature of vampires.

Polidori

The book of Polidori was well-loved however it was over-priced by the 1845-47 edition of Varney the Vampyre, or The Feast of Blood, by James Malcolm Rymer. Much like the Lord Ruthven, Varney is an nobleman who needs blood for survival and would prefer those he kills to be women and younger. This serial, with eight76 pages was the bestselling bestseller of the day and spawned a small market of imitators and productions.

A cover that was the original of the book.

A fresh take on Polidori's as well as Rymer's vampires was revealed in Sheridan le Fanu's Carmilla released in 1872. Carmilla has a feminine vampire that consumes peasant girls in the village nearby and occasionally transforms into the form of a black cat to consume. When

Carmilla encounters the heroine Laura and is in love with her. She then in a very sexualized scene promises to drink her blood to transform into the vampire.

An illustration from the 19th century depicting Carmilla, the female vampire.

Carmilla is confronted by a new symbol in the world of vampire fiction The vampire hunter. Baron Vordenburg is able to track Carmilla to her grave and kills her with an iron stake through her heart and cutting her head off, and burning her body. The remains are then dumped into the river. Carmilla is a source of folklore with many elements, including being the time when vampires come back to his grave during the day or vampirism resulting from taking a suicide decision or being victimized by a vampire and the method used to kill the vampire.

In the year 1897, Bram Stoker published Dracula one of the longest-running and influential of the 19th century vampire novels. When Stoker wrote, the vampire were an integral part of popular literature as well as books about Eastern European folklore were also well-known. Stoker certainly had a fascination with the folklore as Dracula was set in that region, and the vampire is a bit folklore-based with aspects to him for example, like being repulsed by garlic. Stoker added his own twists to the vampire story by creating Dracula capable of turning into a bat, but not appearing in mirrors and having to be welcomed into the home.

Dracula was not just an instant bestseller, but also well written to be part of the canon of literature, but it also had more impact in that it influenced many films (more than 170 by this time). The first one that was influential was Nosferatu that was made in 1922 by the legendary German film director F. W. Murnau. The character of Count Orlok who is played with heavily-madeup in the film by Max Schreck, goes on adventures that are so similar to

Stoker's novel that his family had a successful suit against the company that made the film. The judge ordered to order all film copies were to be destroyed, which meant that this iconic film was gone forever. A few copies survived , and the film was recovered by historians of film. Nosferatu was not just an artistic masterpiece, but it also added a new element to the vampire mythology that was the possibility of being destroyed through exposure to sunlight.

Additional layers were added to Bela Lugosi's commanding performance in the 1931 version of Dracula. His aristocratic manner as well as his exquisite attire the sweeping black cape and his gorgeous Hungarian accent became a staple in the genre of vampires. Incredibly, Universal Studios filmed a Spanish version of the movie in the same period with actors from a different cast, however using identical costumes and sets. The archetype of the vampire was brought to a new set of viewers and the filmmakers who speak Spanish especially in Mexico started to create their own versions of the mythology.

A fascinating effect of this popularity was that it helped keep the myth of actual vampires alive. For instance In England there were only few stories of vampiric spirits during the earlier Middle Ages and these died in the 12th century, however they returned in the 19th century as part of the popularization of literature.

Many writers drew the inspiration for their stories from two true historical characters: Vlad "Dracula" Tepes Also called Vlad the Impaler as well as Lady Bathory. Although neither of them were believed as vampires they're crucial to the myth of vampires.

The Ambras Castle portrait of Vlad III, ca. 1560, is believed to be an exact replica of the original painted during his lifetime.

Bram Stoker based his Count Dracula on the historical character from Vlad Dracula III, who was the prince of Wallachia. Dracula was born in Transylvania in 1431 and lived until 1476 and 1477. His name "Dracula" originates from his father's involvement of the Order of the Dragon, an order of knights that was sworn to cleanse Europe from Muslims and Christian heresies. The father of Vlad II, Vlad II, took the name "Dracul" which means "dragon" to commemorate his membership. Vlad III took the diminutive "Dracula" to honour the memory of his father.

Vlad III lived in a turbulent period in Romanian history, as his country was under the control of the Ottoman Empire was expanding across the Balkans. Vlad Dracula became famous for fighting this Muslim invasion and was considered a feared by the Turks because of his method that involved impaling enemies using stakes that were sharp. Although modern illustrations typically show the person being impaled via in the stomach area, the most popular and painful method was to put the victim in the ground, and the stake would then puncture the vagina or the anus. The weight of the victim would cause them to slide slowly down the stake, with the spike squeezing into the stomach, and eventually taking their life after several hours of pain.

Vlad was also famous in his home country for the severe punishments he inflicted to criminals and those who caused him to be angry. A Russian chronicle, titled The Tale of Dracula from around 1490, describing some of Vlad's wrath: "On one occasion there were ambassadors who came to Vlad, sent from his Turkish ruler. In the process of entering and bowing in accordance with their custom, they refused to take off their hats. heads. Then he asked them: Why do you behave this way? you've come to an eminent ruler, yet you do me the least respect?' they responded: 'That's our custom, sire and it's a norm in our country'. Then he told them: 'I would like to affirm your custom to ensure that you adhere to it with a firm hand'. Then he instructed them that their hats be attached to their heads using tiny iron nails. Then they were released by saying: "Go and inform your leader that he might be accustomed to this disrespect however we aren't accustomed to it, and so it is not appropriate to spread this kind of custom to other kings who are not inclined to follow the custom. Instead, let him stick to the custom within his own your home'."

The sultan of course was at the war over this insult and Vlad's men did their best however, they were overwhelmingly outnumbered and had to be pushed back. Vlad was a strict discipliner with his soldiers. The chronicle states: "He inspected those soldiers who returned from battle. The wounded soldiers from the front received great respect as knights however those who suffered injuries from the rear were impaled with the back with a stake passage. They were greeted by Dracula telling them: "You are not a man , but you are a female'."

The Sultan finally demanded a tribute, and Vlad dazzled him by claiming that he would like to be his vassal, as many of the other Eastern European rulers had done to protect their own skins. Vlad asked for an invitation to meet the Sultan. After five days of marching into Ottoman areas without being harassed then he turned around and began securing towns and cities. "He took captives and killed a lot of men, as well as other Turks whom he impaled. Others were cut in half and burned, including baby suckling babies. He didn't let anyone go. He destroyed the entire country and the Christians came to his homeland and settled the people there. He collected a great amount of booty. When he returned, he gave thanks to the guard of the imperial and left them to say "Go inform the Tsar of what you witnessed. I was able to serve him as efficiently as I could, and should have a desire to serve him again, I'll try to do it similarly in the highest degree of ability. The Tsar was unable to do anything but be slain with dishonor."

In the account, adulterers, criminals and beggars were detained, usually in the castle's courtyard. He seemed to have enjoyed the company of them. "Once he ate lunch under the corpses of people who had died who were buried on stakes. There were a lot of them at the table, but the table was crowded and he took pleasure in his dinner. His server who placed the food in front of him did not like the smell. He rubbed his nose, and then inclined his head. Dracula asked him , 'Why do you have to do that?', and the servant replied, 'Sire, I am unable to bear that smell'. Then Dracula directed the impalement of his servant and said: 'The smell won't reach you after you've been placed on a stake of a higher height.'"

Although he was a sadist, Dracula is revered as an hero in Romania to ensure that the land was free, at the very least for a short period from Ottoman Turks. Dracula's tales of adventure became shocking and popular across Europe and Bram Stoker is known to be influenced by his personal tale. A number of later novels and films also connect Dracula's real Dracula with the famous vampire.

Two very contradicting depictions emerge when contemporary narratives and chronicles are examined. On one hand, the character is depicted in a myriad of sources as a blood-sucking ruler who was fond of inventing unnecessary and cruel punishments. However, on the other hand, he's portrayed as a courageous and brave fight in the face of Ottoman Empire's persistent threat to Wallachian territorial autonomy and sovereignty. There is probably a grain of truth in both accounts; Vlad did indeed implement an internal policy of authoritarians to enhance his influence within the state and he also tried to defend Wallachian autonomy against the Hungarian and Ottoman invasions. However, the accounts are different in every other aspect, such as the particular nature of his punishments as well as the motives behind them, the amount of people who were victims and, perhaps most importantly, the persona of the ruler.

Naturally, the process of determining the identity of who Vlad is and to determine what Vlad really like has become more difficult by the popularity he earned throughout Europe as well as beyond starting with the spread of German as well as Slavic 15th century tales which helped in the creation of a mythical and diabolical persona that was passed through time to present day. Bram Stoker's well-read novel along with the subsequent adaptations of it, created confusion by directly tying the famous beast that haunts South-Eastern Europe, the wampyr as well as the mythological figure in Vlad III Dracula. Today, for the majority of people, Dracula is a reference to Stoker's story, but rarely is the historical figure itself.

Another historical character who has influenced generations of writers about vampires and, consequently, the mythology of the genre, was the Countess of Elizabeth

Bathory of Ecsed often referred to for her role as Lady Bathory. The Hungarian noblewoman lived between 1560/1 and 1614, and was considered to be one of the worst serial killers of women in history.

Bathory

From her seat at Csejte Castle, Lady Bathory quickly began a reign of terror over the local peasant girls. She offered them work as housekeepers and later confined them in prison and subjected them to beatings , as well as other brutal torture. The sadistic side of her made her cut off the flesh of the faces of the victims. Then she began attacking girls of higher rank and this eventually resulted in an investigation.

In 1610 In 1610, Lady Bathory was tried in 1610. Over 300 witnesses and witnesses were present at her trial, and investigators discovered a number of bones and decaying bodies stored inside her house. The charges were for the murder of more than 80 individuals, though some reports claim as many as 700. Three of her attendants were executed for their role in helping with her crime, however she was sentenced throughout her life at Csejte Castle, where she was provided with a series of rooms (the entrance was blocked off, leaving just a tiny opening through which she could get drinks and food). The castle was destroyed just four years later.

Naturally, the tale of the Lady Bathory has evolved in telling. The most well-known tale about her bathing in victim's blood to keep looking youthful - did not appear in the press until 1729, which was a long time after the actual incident.

While neither Vlad or Bathory consumed blood but they have been known as vampires. Sadists from other countries have also been labeled vampires, including Sergeant Francois Bertrand who, in 1849, was found guilty by the French tribunal for digging up fresh corpses , and infringing on their rights. Although this was necrophilia, and not vampirism, the man was named "the Vampire" by the media. The same was the case with Peter Kurten, a German serial rapist and murderer who was called "The Vampire from Dusseldorf". He said he had to look at blood to get an orgasmic experience and claimed to drink his blood from one of the victims. It's disturbing to think that the myth of the vampire could have influenced his horrendous crimes.

Kurten

Chapter 9: Creation Of Vampires: Understanding How Vampires Are Created

"I was a young vampire who was crying at the beauty of the night"

- Louis Interview with the Vampire

The issue of how vampires are born is one that brings up many more questions than the one of the source of vampires. The most evident solution to how vampires were made is the famous bite that transforms a human into a zombie. This is a statement that has some truth in the majority of cases. But the process of creating vampires is much more complicated and complex than a simple bite. The degree of complexity of transformation depends on the nature of the vampire. Is it the creature of literature, legend or mythological? For instance, there are some who believe that vampires from space and other planets can transform a human into a vampire through contact between mouths instead of the usual bite. While we've studied the origins of the term"vampire" from an etymological perspective viewpoint, let me mention that a well-known journalist, Katherine Ramsland, notes that the usage of the term"vampires" is not common to folklore, but it was utilized for the first time in the 16th century. In addition, she states that vampires are compatible with the description of being reanimated bodies that were first seen in 1810 (we have discussed this earlier in our travels with the 3 Englishmen).

Let's revisit the question of how vampires come into existence. One thing we're sure of is that if we look back to the folklore and legends of vampirism and vampires we'll find that the majority of folklore is filled with diverse methods by which a person is able to become vampiric. Based on the mythology and culture the vampiric candidates vary between the seven sons to the seven sons of sinners and criminals as well as children born outside of union, and to a certain in some cases, ladies who allow vampires to look at them. But, for the majority it is just the beginning of a complicated and intricate process of transformation. The process of transformation is solely based on the belief system, culture and belief system that are associated with the legend. Additionally, there are traditions and folklore that consider that the vampires were born with teeth or have an extra nostril. Additionally, certain cultures believe that people who do not receive baptism or those that are born on the holy day are potential candidates for vampirism.

Stories of vampires say that if you're on the floor of a ballroom with the vampire of your dreams and he is watching you, it is likely that he will make you their companion and, in some cases it could be a sexual partner. In this case the interested vampire is your maker, creator or your parent. If you're a film enthusiast then you'll know that this kind of transformation is largely dependent on the capacity of the vampire's parent to keep from revealing the desire for the blood's essence.

In actual fact it is the act of taking the blood of a tiny amount from a deceased person with the sole intention of creating a brand new vampire requires a lot of caution from the vampire who is the parent. If taken in small amounts the blood supply of a person can provide a vampire with enough energy for an extended period of duration without causing death to the person who was killed.

Furthermore, depending on the kind of vampire, the process of turning a human to a vampire, or what we call crossing over , or bringing, may trigger a variety of reactions from the vampire. For instance, the new vampire could be able to glimpse the memories as well as thoughts and memories of the vampire who was their parent. Certain newborn vampires might revel in the development of supernatural abilities. An excellent example can be found in the Interview with the Vampire, written of Anne Rice where Louis, an actual vampire, recounts the story of how he was transformed into vampire through Lestat at the age of 1791. In the book, you will find an extremely vivid account of paralysis inability to speak and complete fear that can occur after the process of crossing over.

When we conclude this chapter, we need to highlight a key aspect. The majority of the vampires we encounter in the folklore do not look like the white-skinned, flawless, and radiant supernatural beings that we are used to seeing as the avatar of vampires. The majority of them are reconstructed corpses in various states of disarray and decay.

We now have a complete understanding of the steps involved in making vampires, let's examine another aspect of this process: being born a child who has both a vampire and human parent.

Chapter 10: Half Breed Vampire Children And Immortal Children

"Half mortal half immortal. It was conceived and carried by the baby when she was still a human."

"AroFrom dawn breaking Part 2

In the history of mankind, there have been numerous instances in which humans and vampires forged their relationship. Although the idea of a half breed immortality - half human and half vampire children isn't a common occurrence in the pages of folklore about vampires in the past, there are numerous instances when both male vampires and human female have shared an infant. The result of this arrangement are a half-breed infant also known as hybrid. In general, vampires are not able to create. So the half breed is very rare. In the novel (and film) Breaking Dawn, only five hybrid vampires are found (Renesmee, Nahuel, Jennifer, Maysun, and Serena). In the film the film, all hybrid vampires share characteristics of both vampires and humans.

From a historical point an historical point of concept for a hybrid a bit elusive. It could be because the entire procedure is fraught with controversy. But let's examine the details we can gather today. According to the majority of vampire stories the vulnerability of humans can make the whole process of hybridization very risky and challenging. The concept of a hybrid is only possible when a female is sexually involved with male vampires. You can tell this is an act which male vampires are more likely to be willing to take on, since being able to avoid killing humans or drinking their essence is difficult for most vampires. So, the idea of the hybrid child requires a great deal of self-control, especially given the sexual intimacy of the process.

In the event that a man vampire could successfully mat with a female who is human, without killing her, and then effectively impregnate the female, the fetus within the woman isn't typical fetuses. First, it develops faster than an ordinary human fetus. Additionally, the fetus could also cause a lot of stress to the mother before giving birth. That means that when the fetus grows within the womb of the mother, it may grow to be very strong and eventually result in harming or even killing the mother. In the film Breaking Dawn, part one we see a hint of the kind of diet that the hybrid prefers. In the film in which Bella is the female lead is pregnant, her fetus will not prefer human food (Bella throws up every food she eats). But when she drinks blood, she improves and stronger (even when the fetus does end to kill her). Also, in the movie the fetus is full-on after just a month of conception. Although there might be some truth in thisstory, there's not much to add to this. In addition, when the fetus reaches the age of maturity during the womb, it makes use of the vampire power and teeth to escape its mother's body. It often causes dying the mommy. It's also impossible to prove that the only solution for a mother to be saved when the fetus has ripped her heart is to inject her with vampire venom and transforming her into a new vampire. According to the film Breaking Dawn, only one mother has survived the hybrid conception process and birthing process.

The anatomy and physiology of hybrids

As we said previously, hybrid vampire children get the most beneficial from both sides i.e. they inherit certain traits from their human and vampire parents. Since most vampires are gorgeous they are also (superficially) gorgeous. The beauty and power and strength of vampires implies that other vampires could be mistaken for immortal youngsters (immortal children are children of humans that are bitten, and then transformed into vampire infants). They're very risky because they are unable to control their cravings for blood or conceal their vampire identity hidden).

The primary difference between the hybrid vampire and "normal vampire" is the fact that the hybrid is equipped with functioning hearts and blood coursing through its veins (although their hearts beat more quickly than humans). In contrast to vampires who are bitten hybrids are also capable of sleeping and obtaining nutrition from human food and blood. In the same film, Renesmee is a hybrid child. It has a skin that only lightly and slowly illuminates under direct sun in contrast to the normal skin of a vampire, which sparkles and glows as diamonds when subjected direct sunlight.

Because humans and vampires share particular scents and scent, hybrid vampires are an amalgamation of both scents. They are unique in that they're balanced between the two scents that make them attractive to both vampires and humans. According to legend, hybrid vampires possess 24 chromosomes pair. Many believe that this is caused by an chromosome rearrangement, or perhaps an error in sampling. There isn't much information regarding a hybrid's capacity to reproduce. In the case of female hybrids, reproduction is possible, given that the reason female vampires are unable to reproduce is due to their inability to alter and adapt to the female fetus.

The development of hybrid vampires can be quick in the initial stages. They are fully mature at seven years old (look like mature teenagers at this point). But, when they reach the age of seven the body stops becoming a complete stopper and are in an ageless state similar to other vampires.

In terms of abilities as well as abilities, they possess the same abilities as the 'normal vampire'. They are more powerful than humans and have more attuned senses, and are more agile than humans of average age. However, the hybrid's powers and senses are more dull than the vampire's. Hybrids have an excellent memory recall and a brain which develops faster as they get older (hybrids can speak in full sentences or walk for a few days or even weeks after the time they were born). Additionally, to date there's been no evidence of hybrids being venomous. In the book, Breaking Dawn part 2 it is apparent that there is an incongruity to this assertion in the character of Nahuel who is believed to be poisonous. In addition, hybrid vampires like pure breed vampires can also heal. In the event of a dismemberment only male hybrid vampires is able to heal and repair itself since female hybrid vampires appear lacking the venom component essential to facilitate the super-healing process. Although the above assertion is the truth, there is an underlying belief about female hybrids as well as their venomous condition. For instance, in the Breaking Dawn book series, Renesmee and Nahuel's three sisters get their unique traits from their human mother and hence their lack of poison. However, Nahuel has a hybrid male appears to have acquired most of his characteristics through his vampire dad, and hence his venomous condition.

We've discussed a central element of the myth of vampires it is time to consider a different, equally important aspect that is vampires and werewolves. Before we get to this, let's examine hybrid facts as explained in the work of Professor George Gutsche, a professor at the University of Arizona where he has taught a class on vampires and werewolves over the past five years. The professor provides an extremely detailed insight into the characteristics of hybrids and their role in history , and the mythology of vampires.

The professor claims that the majority of the information we have about the human-vampire offspring comes out of Southeastern Europe, the Balkan region, to be exact. The Balkan region is where words like Dhampir, Vampirdzhiya, Glog Vampirovic, Dhampir and Svetocher are all utilized to refer to the descendants of the human vampire tying. Additionally, in folklore, hybrids possess special abilities, including the ability to identify and eliminate shape shifters which are not detectable for other vampires. In most folklores the vampire of the common folklore cannot transform into the form of a bat. However, they possess the unique ability to disguise themselves as pumpkins. Further studies into this reveal that hybrids don't possess the burning desire for blood, or possess the immortality of undead vampires. In addition, in the majority of lore vampires like Dracula (as depicted in the Bram Stockers novel) expose themselves to sunlight. But this doesn't necessarily mean that they are drawn to darkness. Hybrids however do not have any more affinity for darkness than humans do.

If we examine hybrids from a professor's point of view one question that comes into play: does a hybrid feel an affinity with either their vampire or human counterparts? If we look at the mythology of the past, we can see that hybrids are more like humans because, unlike typical vampire (reanimated corpses) they live (they carry blood through their veins). This is why the majority of vampires are averse of hybrids. In addition, to people, hybrids have become brand new attractive phenomenon (especially due to their ability to kill vampires who have reanimated). It is crucial to note that in most folklores hybrids are males who are considered to be special in the community due to their ability to recognize normal vampires. In certain folklores there are references to female hybrids (a great illustration could be The Breaking Dawn book series).

Additionally, in folklore, there is a contradiction that pops up. We are of the opinion that the hybrid offspring is an element of danger towards the mom, the folklore doesn't agree with this belief (there are no references to this risk in the majority of folklore). However, in the majority of these folktales it is said that dad (the vampire dad) poses a risk to the mother since he is coming to her every night, and draining her of her vitality every night can cause her death. Furthermore, in contrast to the myth that was retold in the well-known Breaking Dawn series, in folklore there is no mention of an acceleration in pregnancy. Actually, throughout the majority of the tales we've looked at, the accounts mention the full nine months of pregnancy.

Chapter 11: Vampires And Werewolves: The Age Long Enmity

"We're all sustained by the power of magic, Sookie. My magic is just a little different than yours, that's all."

Bill - True Blood

Vampires are a common theme throughout books, lore and the big screen are always able to refer to another mythical creature called the werewolf. A lycanthrope or a werewolf is an imaginary creature which can change between being half human and half wolf. In the fictional world that we live in werewolves are an integral component of any vampire tale films, stories, or movies written. Modern literature through literature, art and movies always pits vampires and werewolves up against one the other. For instance in the film Underworld the conflict between the two groups is an all-out battle. The trilogy is woven around the war that is waged between lycans with the vampires. In the other writings and films like True Blood and Twilight, the animosity between them appears to intensify, though in various ways. For instance in Twilight there are two i.e. werewolves and vampires create physical borders and treaties that differentiate and divide from each other despite sharing the same land with humans. When asked about the reasons behind that, Stephanie Meyer, the author of the Twilight book series, says that the main reason for the hatred lies in the fact that the cold ones also known as vampires are fond of killing werewolves, which is why their existence is a continuation of the creation of werewolves. In the novel (Twilight novel series) the origin or more precisely, the evolution of werewolves occurs due to the increasing presence of vampires. Further, in the book and film, the 'becoming-a-werewolf-process' is noble, self-sacrificial and almost unavoidable (due to the presence of the cold ones).

It's not enough to provide the answer to the crucial question of why vampires and werewolves antagonists according to the majority of stories? Although this is important however, it's not something I can answer in just one straightforward phrase or sentence. But, if you're avidly pursuing the genre of vampires, you'll be aware that the majority of contemporary vampire stories tend to feature werewolves and vampires in the same arch enemies. Every author uses their own unique style of writing to take a different twist on the rivalry between these two mythological creatures. In certain stories, the animosity is a result of a battle for prey. In other stories, the animosity comes in the need to defend humans, who are their natural prey (as for instance, in the Quileute werewolves of Twilight). Twilight novel series). In some stories and instances the authors weave their stories to portray a feud that has been brewing for centuries between the two mythological creatures. With so many writers adding their own twist on the obvious rivalry between these two species, there's very little information about how the war started. Let's look at one story that comes from Encyclopedia Mythallica, a site which is dedicated to myths.

The website states that long time in the past, werewolves and vampires weren't at war. They actually were in perfect harmony with the myths and beliefs of the human race. According to the legend that a hybrid maiden was born to be (there is a lack of details about the process of her creation). The maiden brought the two creatures together, and was the ultimate symbol of the alliance between two species. Then , chaos ensued. The woman was killed (again it is unclear why this happened, and there is no information on what caused this to happen, however it did happen). The death led to finger pointing while both species blamed one the other. The result was a long conflict in which both species vowed to kill each other upon sight.

From a fictional perspective i.e. when we consider any fictional work into consideration there isn't any real alternative, correct or incorrect way to explain or comprehend the conflict between the two different species (as we have said earlier, every author makes use of the conflict to create their own interpretation and narrative). If we take a look at the numerous fictional works and films that pit against the two species, it's simple to understand the reason why these two species are an exciting adversaries on screen or paper. They are both formidable creatures of the night that have no predators known to them, other than the other. If we consider the fight from a folklore and mythological standpoint there is little or evidence to suggest that the two species have been in previous interactions. In reality, there is no mythology that describes how the two creatures interact. Furthermore, many writings about vampires do not mention werewolves in any way. This suggests that if they were mortal enemies, like the majority of stories, films and plays suggest that they were, there would be evidence of the conflict in the books of history. It does not in any means mean that the conflict between the two is not mythological in the sense of. It isn't the situation. It is vital to remember that both species attempt to remain hidden from humankind. This means there might exist a trace of interactions between them somewhere.

Despite the animosity that we witness between them, whether in the movies or in those pages in your most loved vampire or werewolf book from a fictional standpoint there have been instances when the two are able to cooperate for the benefit of humankind. An excellent example is the Twilight book series , where Cullen's, as well as the Quileute werewolves cooperate to defend Bella and their community yet they retain their desire to kill one another. Maybe I should point out that most of the time like vampires, they do not have the capacity to be independent i.e. their decisions are governed by the demands of a pack, and an individual leader.

The vampires and werewolves' rivalry takes on a more friendly character during Twilight (in some instances), Twilight books (in certain instances) but the same feud has a totally different angle when it comes to True Blood. For True Blood, the rivalry is more violent. In True Blood, the Southern Vampire Mysteries area has some restrictions. In the show, vampires are limited to nighttime, as opposed to Twilight where vampires are able to go out during the daytime. What this means is that there's a chance that the battle between werewolves and vampires is tilted towards the one hand i.e. that of the werewolves since their ability to move through the daylight means that they are able to hunt vampires and sleep inside their coffins. Additionally, of the two, the belief waswolves will be more aggressive of them all.

Another fantastic example of the vampire war between the werewolves that is currently in the spotlight is The BBC's Being Human Show that depicts the two sides as mortal adversaries. But, unlike the previous shows we reviewed the show takes an entirely different approach. In particular, unlike the Twilight book series , where werewolves and vampires seem to be equal in their battles In this show, vampires appear to be the dominant species as they frequently fight werewolves and earn profits from them through cage fights. Furthermore, the show is a story about vampires and werewolves living in peace, and even a ghost into the mix. Despite their love for one another There are numerous instances where werewolves and vampires are depicted in different light and with opposing perspectives. This is a bit contradictory since in some ways, the two creatures should be lifelong companions since they are among the most popular mythical creatures known to mankind (loathed and adored, worshipped and hunted almost in equal proportions). Most of the time the conflict is due to the essence that both of them represents. The behaviors and desires of vampires are primitive. But, it is evident that werewolves are a symbol of this in the most literal appearance.

We have previously examined the transformation into a vampire from a

148

human. The transformation between human and vampire, and human to werewolf do show an interesting distinction. In particular when the transformation to vampire is mostly focused on the face (and minor changes to the body aren't noticed) however, the transformation to a werewolf is incredibly physical, as the entire body transforms into something totally different from the human that was originally. In reality, in the majority of stories, the term "dog is often utilized as a reference to the hierarchical nature of werewolves as pack animals that resemble wild dogs, regardless of their obvious physical resemblances. As opposed to the vampire which is an aspirational, and even sexual creature that is sexually attractive, there is a significant difference , particularly when you consider that the werewolf is considered to be an evil creature that is far removed from the human form. However the distinction between the two is apparent; a vampire can offer the glamour of immortality, while a is a creature with constraints and rules that are quite similar to the normal human lifestyle.

With a solid grasp of the alleged conflict between werewolves and vampires (the use of the word "alleged" wasps is very deliberate) Now we can look at a different aspect of vampires that we need to look into.

Chapter 12: Vlad The Impaler Aka Count Dracula

"We Draculs have the claim to pride..."I am only one of my kind"

Dracula - Dracula in Bram Stoker's Dracula

Of all vampires of all vampires, Count Dracula is possibly the most well-known. It is possibly because of Dracula's Bram Stockers 1897 gothic horror novel of the same name. Bram's novel is probably the first time the idea of the count was accepted by the mainstream. The book tells the story of Dracula's quest to move towards England in Transylvania in the hope of spreading the curse of undead. The story also describes the battle between Dracula and an enclave of human beings headed by professor Abraham Van

Helsing. While Bram's story is fictional however, it shouldn't surprise anyone to find out that Vlad the Impaler was an actual person (whether or whether he actually was a vampire remains to be determined).

The evidence suggests that the well-known Dracula was the famous Count Dracula has been Vlad III, the Prince of Wallachia from 1431 to 1477. He lived in the Draculesti's house which is part of the Basarab house of Basarab. The Draculesti is also said to use other names, including Vlad Dracula and Vlad Draculea. He was three times Voivode-of-Wallachia , and was a ruler at the period of Ottoman victory over the Balkans. The father of his was Vlad II Dracul and was an officer of the Order of the Dragon which was a group that was established within Eastern Europe to protect Christians as well as Christianity. In Romania the Vlad III is a folk hero because of his position as a protector active for Romanians from the north and south of Danube. A large number of Romanian ordinary folk and nobles (boyars) have migrated across Danube to Wallachia because of the rule of Vlad and his most often successful battles on the Ottomans.

The reputation of the "impaler is primarily due to the practice of impaling his adversaries. In his time and during his reign the man was a gruesome savage. His cruelty was reported quickly throughout Germany as well as Europe. Since then, few have brought more terror in the hearts of people than his. The legend of Dracula as portrayed by Dracula as written and told in Bram's tale has been an inspiration to numerous horror and vampire stories from all over the globe , while also being a source of horror for a lot of people. As we've mentioned before, the Dracula, although fictional, has been like a real person. In addition the real Count Vlad III was famous for his love for blood. But it is true that Bram was a model for his Count Vlad according to numerous historians who have examined the connection between the two men There is almost there being any connection between the two.

The real stories of Vlad III

Many accounts say Vlad was born in 1431. Vlad was born around 1431 in what is simply refer to as present Transylvania the central region of modern-day Romania. Based on Florin Curta who is a professor of medieval archaeology and history in the University of Florida, the connection with Vlad Impaler's birth and Transylvania is disputed. In Bram's tale he refers to the count as Transylvania. But, there is no evidence of Vlad having any property in Transylvania. In actual fact, as per Curta the modern-day tourist attraction is regarded as the Vlad's castle was not ever the home of Vlad, the Wallachian prince. The primary reason that it is thought to be the most likely home for a vampire is that it is a perfect fit for our notion of what a castle built by a vampire could appear to be (the castle is situated atop an eerie mountain and is spooky in every way). It is clear that Vlad III did not even step his foot in the castle, let alone owned the castle or reside there.

One possible reason for this mythical idea could be the reality that Vlad's father Vlad II, owned a house in Sighisoara in Transylvania. But, there's an ambiguity about the fact that Vlad III was born there. It is, however, possible since all indications indicate to suggest that Vlad III was born in Targoviste in the year 1798, which at that time was the seat of royal power of Wallachia. Vlad's father, who was Voivode or ruler at the period.

According to the historical writings According to the scripts of history, according to the scripts of history, King Sigismund in Hungary (who then became Holy Roman Emperor) inducted Vlad II into the legendary Order of the Dragon in 1431. This was the reason why he gave the older Vlad name or his surname Dracul that comes from the Romanian word , drac, which means dragon. If you go to present time Romania the word drac refers to a frightful creature, the devil. The dragon's order that the two Vlad's were happy to be a part of, had a single goal or goal: the destruction of the Ottoman empire, also known as the Turkish. So, Wallachia, the home principality of Vlad situated in the middle of Europe, both Christian Europe as well as the Muslim regions in the Ottoman Empire was the scene for bloody and horrific fights between two sides.

Vlad in captivity

The year 1442 was the time Vlad II was called to a meeting of diplomatic relations together with the Sultan Murad II. Vlad II was invited to join Radu along with Vlad III along with him. The encounter turned out be a scam and the three were detained and held hostage. Vlad II was released , but only when he was able to leave his sons at home. The Sultan's motive for keeping the sons was to make sure that Vlad II acted in a manner that was acceptable to the war that was raging that was raging between Hungary as well as Turkey. This is the opinion of Elizabeth Miller, a professor in the emeritus department and researcher in the Memorial University of Newfoundland Canada.

While in captivity, the two brothers i.e. Vlad III and Radu had instruction in science, the arts and the philosophy. Vlad was a highly proficient warrior and horseman According to Raymond McNally and Radu Florescu who have written numerous books about Vlad III. In captivity the two brothers were given a fair amount of respect. But, the confinement irked Vlad and his brother relented and joined his Turkish side. Vlad's animosity grew, and it became the driving force in his battle to the Turks.

While the two children were held captive while the older Vlad was engaged in a battle to maintain his position and title of the Voivode of Wallachia. The year 1447 saw him fell in the fight and was removed as head of Wallachia by the local boyars. Vlad and Vlad's older half-brother Mircea were later executed in the swamps around Balteni (a location that lies in to Bucharest in Romania and Targoviste in modern-day Romania).

in 1448 Vlad III launched a aggressive campaign in order to take back the seat of his father. In the year 1448, the leader at the time was Vladislav II. According to Curta's account the first time he tried the throne of Vladislav II was based on military assistance from Ottoman city governors that were located along the Danube River. The king also took advantage of the of the fact that, during when he launched his assault, Vladislav had gone to the Balkans to combat against the Ottomans to take on Governor of Hungary who was John Hunyadi. While he was able to regain the throne of his father and sacked, his tenure as leader of Wallachia was only a short. He was deposed within two months after Vladislav returned to take back his throne in Wallachia with the assistance of Hunyadi.

Following his defeat, which occurred between 1448 and 14156, there's no record of Vlad's movements. There is evidence that he switched sides during the

Hungarian-Ottoman war. He renounced his connections to the Ottoman Governors in Danube cities. Danube cities and entered into an alliance with the King Ladislaus V Hungary who's dislike of Vladislav II of Wallachia was as strong as the dislike of Vlad.

After the decline of Constantinople in 1453, Vlad III military and political skills truly came to the limelight. After the fall of Constantinople in 1453, the Ottomans were well-positioned to take over the entire continent of Europe. Since Vlad was a strong anti-Ottoman stand, he later declared the Voivode or ruler of Wallachia in 1456. The first thing he did was to cease paying any annual interest to Ottoman sultan. Ottoman Sultan (a measure originally designed to maintain that peace was maintained between Ottomans as well as Wallachia).

Vlad the Impaler's legend Vlad the Impaler

To strengthen his power as the voivode in Wallachia, Vlad III needed to end the long-running historical disputes with Wallachia's boyars. Wallachia boyars. The legend goes that Vlad brought hundreds of Boyars for a banquet meal, aware that they could challenge his authority. At the time of the party the guests were wounded and their twitching bodies impaled by spikes which earned him the title Vlad Impaler. This incident is one of the many occasions that gave him the posthumous name for Vlad the Impaler.

It isn't clear whether any of the tales concerning Vlad or his immoral talents were true. It is uncertain, particularly considering that a lot of the pamphlets that detailed these stories were written with a hostile attitude towards Vlad III. It is nevertheless important to mention that the vast majority of pamphlets that were printed at the time contain an equally horrific story of Vlad. This is enough to believe that the majority of the tales about Vlad III were historically accurate and precise. There are a few of these tales in the book of 1490 "The Tale of Dracula," written by monks. The book depicts Vlad III as a just but brutal ruler.

Vlad legend causes fear in the hearts of many. Vlad legend is believed to have imprisoned numerous Saxon merchants, who were allies to the boyars of Kronstad during 1456. Additionally in the same year, i.e. 1456, a few Ottoman representatives who had an meeting with Vlad refused to take off their turbans, citing customs of their religion. According to legend, Vlad was praised for their religious fervor and ordered their turbans of religious significance pinned to their skulls and heads.

After Mehmet II defeated Constantinople and conquered Wallachia during 1462. He made his way across Wallachia's capital Targoviste and found it empty, save for the bodies impaled of Ottoman soldiers Vlad had been able to capture.

Vlad's death Vlad

Following the impalement in the Ottoman POW in the month of August 1462 Vlad III was forced into exile in Hungary. In a position of no match against his foe Mehmet II,, Vlad, was imprisoned for a couple of years in exile. He was got married and had two kids. Radu Vlad's younger brother who was a partisan of those who sided with the Ottomans throughout the War, took charge of the administration of Wallachia following Vlad was exiled. When the elder brother, i.e. Radu passed away in 1475 the majority of the boys and rulers of various municipalities favored Vlad in the reign of Wallachia.

In 1476, with the assistance from Stephen III The Great, the voivode of Moldavia, Vlad made a last effort to return to his throne as the ruler of Wallachia. While he succeeded however, his time on the throne was only short-lived. The same year, on an expedition to fight against Vlad and the Ottomans, Vlad and his small, vanguard-sized soldier fell victim to an ambush at which Vlad was killed. This brings up a fundamental question Where is the burial site of Vlad the third?

There has been a lot of controversy over the place of Vlad III's burial site. Some believe that Vlad III was burial in the church of the monastery in Snagov located on the northern end of the present day Bucharest in line with burial traditions of the past. However, recent research by historians have challenged the notion that Vlad's burial location could be in his former home, the Monastery of Comana located between Danube and Bucharest (this is close to the location believed to be Vlad's final battle).

The difference between Vlad's true life and Stoker's version of the count Dracula highlights the crucial question what happens to vampires and how do you get rid of one? We will address this question in the following chapter. But, it is crucial to note that contrary to Stoker's version regarding Dracula, Vlad III did actually die.

Chapter 13: How To Destroy or Kill A Vampire

"I'm Gentleman Death dressed in lace and silk I'm here to light the candles. The heart of the canker is the heart of the rose."

--Anne Rice,The Vampire Lestat

In Hollywood and in the world of fiction There are many different theories of how to cause the demise of a vampire, be it full breed or pure. These are the places where myths like those about the killing of a stake in the heart, or by the application of a crucifix or garlic as seen in the film Van Helsing arise. Additionally, folklore and history has a wealth of stories of ways to kill some of the cold creatures or even the undead. In the Twilight books the only way that for a vampire to die is by cutting off their head and burning it. In other works of fiction vampires be killed or disintegrate due to the direct exposure to sunlight. There are myths that describe the death of the undead being caused by being immersed in running water and countless other instances of death caused by the rub of a garlic-scented stake into the heart of the creature.

It might come as an unexpected surprise to some of you to find out that the majority of these murders are actually based on truth in the real stories. But, there is no any doubt that some of the methods of killing have fallen victim to the imagination of mankind and therefore are not a viable method to eliminate any undead. It is true that contemplating ways you could kill undead doesn't necessarily mean that any of these strategies will be effective if you had to meet a vampire in the present. In all likelihood, as the oldest of creatures, they are bound to have come up with methods to protect themselves from being killed by such items as garlic stakes that go to the heart. However, we must explore the deep depths of what it takes to prevent a demise in the hands of humans.

Find her Her Home

The majority of folklore holds that vampires are the most vulnerable during their sleep in bed, which, according to these stories is the case during the day, since vampires tend to be sceptical of sunshine (perhaps because they're creatures of darkness). So, it's reasonable to consider or even conclude that when one i.e. the intended killer of vampires can discover a place where vampires live the vampire at issue might be in serious trouble. However finding the haven of a vampire is only the beginning. They guard their sleep places very well. Folklore has stories of vampires being accompanied by Ghouls to watch over their sleeping places in the daytime (there are some believing that entire war between werewolves and vampires was due to the fact that vampires had enslaved werewolves, and employed them as their guards in the day, until werewolves revolted). Additionally, if a killer is able to locate the vampire's hideout the vampire killer has to be alert for the booby traps. Furthermore, because vampires love the dark, their dwellings or hideaways could be covered in darkness. So, even with guards removed there is an opportunity that the vampire could awake before the slayer is able to kill to kill the vampire (there is plenty of debate about the idea of whether vampires sleep).

Take a stake in the heart

The act of staking a vampire is the oldest method for paralyzing the vampire. The emphasis is on the paralysis aspect since the stake placed in a vampire's heart doesn't end its life. In fact, if are a fan of vampires, you've probably noticed in the majority of books and films removal of the stake is a way to bring back that vampire (with all memories of those who harmed it). A stake placed in the center of the body is an option when no other means of stopping or incapacitating the vampire is in place. Furthermore, once the vampire is impaled using it, it could be buried behind a wall or submerged in concrete so that, should the stake be rotten and the vampire is revived the vampire, they is also able to escape from the second tomb or prison.

Make sure that he/she is protected against his/her

In most cases it's nearly impossible to take down a vampire by poison. But, if is guarded by Ghouls and other creatures of the mortal realm like minions, it is possible to reduce the support for the vampire by removing the vampire's agents or even killing them. This will ensure that your vampire's system of support deteriorates. If there is no support system, it's then much easier to end the life of the vampire. Be aware that just because a vampire's system of support is not strong, does not necessarily mean that the vampire is weaker.

Hacking and cutting

Chopping and hacking are the most well-known medieval methods to kill vampires. Therefore, they are the most simple techniques. Although vampires heal and recover quicker than humans, they can inflict enough damage to the vampire that the wound can be severe enough to cause death. The major issue with this type of killing is that it's impossible to control the act of inflicting these kinds of wounds, especially when the vampire is a powerful creature that is capable of inflicting death. It is crucial to note that this type of attack is nearly impossible to execute by just one person (unless they have an intention to commit suicide). Thus, the most effective strategy to destroy vampires is an approach that is targeted and is followed by cutting away at the vampire's bodily components after he or she becomes in a state of unconsciousness.

Find out the secret of the vampire's life

The existence of a vampire is contingent on the ability of the vampire to be a part of the normal world (if you look back at the mythology we've studied over the years you'll see that there have been numerous instances in which people die by the wrath of a mob just because they were believed to have been vampires). It is therefore possible to create a outrage in a mob by disclosing the vampire's secrets. In the Twilight books There is a flashback which reveals how Carlisle escapes from an angry mod for a few minutes after being turned into a baby.

Death through fire

Fire is a favorite among vampire hunters for a method to snare and destroy the living creatures. It is possibly because fire is easy to get and vampires are averse to its presence (and are prone towards it).

Death by the light of dawn

The sun's rays are perhaps the most widely used method for destroying the undead. But, unlike fire, which is simple to handle sunlight is dependent on the natural world. In contrast unlike fire, which is not difficult to extinguish and countermeasure but sunlight isn't. In popular mythology, vampires make every step to make sure that sunlight in the morning or at any other time is not able to be able to catch them on their feet and without a escape route or hiding spot. It is nearly impossible to catch the vampire unprepared. If the hunter of vampires fights the beast at night, they may stall until dawn. Once the rays of the dawn sun shine across the sky, hunters could gain some advantage against the vampire, who would then be more focused on being able to hide against the sunlight.

Cannibalism

In the books, history or films and even folklore There are many instances in which certain vampires hunt other vampires. In this instance the most effective method for the vampire hunting hunter to defeat another vampire is through diablerie. It is the act of drinking blood from a victim or vampire and consuming their soul and blood in the process. It is crucial to remember that diablerie is among the most heinous crimes committed by vampires. But, it can be motivating because the devourer gets more powerful and can manifest certain of his/her victims' abilities and discipline.

A history lesson for the future A brief history of the vampire slaying kits

Vampires and their mythology have been around for a long period of. Vampire hunters and vampire slayers like Van Helsing and Buffy the vampire slayer are also around since the time vampires have existed. Contrary to other myths that have been told throughout history one of the main reasons that make the myth of the vampire extremely appealing and intoxicating is the fact that vampires, though immortal creatures can be defeated, and even killed (as we have seen earlier) by using the different methods and tools that we mentioned earlier. This is a significant junction. The majority of folklore, films and books describe the use of certain objects and tools for the pursuit and destruction vampires. If you have read a lot of these stories something will come forth: A vampire killing kit, also known as a the vampire hunting kit.

As of now, it is difficult to determine the very first time that a hunting kit was employed to hunt or kill an animal. But, according to the majority of sources, the majority of what we think of as a vampire killing kit was created by an entrepreneur at the beginning of the 19th and the 20th century. The person (his name isn't mentioned in mythology or folklore) recognized that the publication of Bram's work meant that vampires and their nature would become a hot topic for quite a long period of. Also, it's impossible to find the very first use of a vampire slaying tool and let alone the very first person who used it. However, this doesn't suggest that vampire-slaying kit will not have a place in the lore of vampires.

It was an unidentified entrepreneurial person who developed the idea of kits for killing vampires; there is a rumor that communication to the time of 1800 was sporadic and extremely difficult, many readers of Bram's book, Dracula believed it as a genuine account , and believed it was believed that Castle Dracula in Transylvania was actually an actual castle. With this information and the myth of the vampires, as described in the book by Stocker to design an easy, stylish and effective kit to kill vampires to be used by the regular Transylvanian and American traveler who believed that Dracula and his gang as described in the book were indeed real. The kit would include everything one would need to keep vampires out and protect themselves in the event that it was necessary. And it was then that the modern-day vampire killing kit was born.

According to rumours and by the stories of the modern kits for slaying vampires, the original kits contained everything you need. It included:

-Stake

The Holy Bible

Garlic oil or garlic

Pistol and accessories

- Crucifix

- A secret liquid which was to be consumed in the event that one were to be attacked by vampires.

The designer of these kits , who wanted to remain anonymous, created an anonymous pseudonym, Professor Blomberg. The kits were more like medical-type kits that were from the Victorian time. They had a clean finish and were stored in a wooden container which was ideal to display. In spite of this there are a segment that believes the idea of vampire killing kits dates in early in the Middle Ages. As of now, there is no evidence that suggests that there were vampire killing kits during the middle ages.

Additionally, there is a section in the community who think the idea of kits for slaying vampires originated from a gun dealer who owned a few old pistols which no longer functioned. In the effort to package the pistols again and sell the guns they came up with vampire slaying kits that showcase the guns and other components inside the package. Due to the contradictory nature of these claims as well as the fact there's only a few sources of information in regards to kits for slaying vampires It's difficult to determine the source of the kits.

What's inside a vampire killing kit

It is vital to keep in mind that various kits for killing vampires could contain different components. Here are most well-known standards and the items included in a standard kit for slaying vampires.

A cross-stake or two, or hand-sharpened stakes of wood

A bottle, or two boxes of rock salt

*A strong knife

*One holy Rosary

A pamphlet that explains how to identify the signs of a vampire

One large, two small bottles of holy water

Silver chain

There are several maps of the region that you will be searching

*A box should contain at the very least two garlic cloves

One candle with matches (for use in cellars and crypts that are darkened)

One mirror to test the reflection of a vampire that you suspect

*A Holy Bible and a ready copy of the Exorcism Prayer

*One coffin nail sachet (to keep the vampire sealed inside its coffin)

Apart from the above-mentioned items larger kits for slaying vampires could also include these items:

A pistol- it is ideal to buy a pistol with silver or wood bullets

*Your Last Will and Testament, and your funeral instructions in the event of your death.

*A bone saw

*A consecrated earth box or bottle

*An Axe

* A spyglass

A box of wafers for communion

* Tooth pliers

A bottle of sand fine-grain

* Field glasses

*An oil lamp

*A Compass

Chapter 14: Through the Pages Of History: The Story Of Vampires As Mythical Creatures

"There is something about vampires that is sexy. The same reason is why women gravitate towards the bad guy- you are drawn to them but should not be able to"

- Nina Dobrev

Before we can identify vampires' place in history, we have to first understand this mythical animal. According to Wikipedia the term "vampire" refers to a mythical creature , whose existence and survival depends on their ability to eat the blood of living beings i.e. sucking blood from the living creature. In addition, according to the same source the vampire who is dead that which we see today (along with the other vampires) visited the loved ones of theirs killed and caused a lot of trouble (well it's in the legends of folklore). In many cases, the monster we fear and love with the same breath, wore shrouds which people typically refer to as having a dark or ruddy appearance and was also bloated. As you can see from this lengthy account of the early vampires, the idea of vampires, their appearance and appear and behave is quite different from the notion of vampires that we are accustomed to in the present. This raises one important issue that we try to find out the answer to in the event that the mythology or folklore about vampires goes evolving with time, who's to determine if this is true or not.

The mythological nature of vampires isn't an original concept. The creature that we discussed above was first mentioned in the 1800s. Additionally, note should be given to the fact that even the just the mention of vampires dates farther back than that and there are records from many cultures suggesting the existence of vampires at some time or another. The popularity of the term vampire as a term wasn't until the 18th century, when there was an the emergence of vampire mythology that spread throughout Western Europe and other areas of Europe where legends about vampires were prevalent and ad nauseam. In this regard, it is crucial to mention that, while the legend of vampires was a common theme in these areas however, local variations of the vampire had various names. For instance the mythical vampire that we now know as called Vrykolakas and Strigoi in Greece as well as Strigoi within Romania. In a way this aspect of vampirism and its nature has heightened the amount of superstition that exists in Europe as well as other regions of the globe that can be described as hysteria, to the degree that led to the actual stacking of dead bodies of those who are accused of being vampires.

At the beginning of the development of vampires, the mythological nature of vampires was difficult to differentiate. Perhaps this is due to the simple reality that in the beginning days, there were a lot of instances of innocent people suffer from porphyria, a rare inherited or acquired disorder of specific enzymes which participate with the production of both heme as well as poryphyrins. These disorders manifested as neurologic problems, skin issues and even both within the heart.

But, in the present vampires and vampirism as creatures are mostly mythological and fictional in the natural world. But, despite our advancement in knowledge and the ability to discern between fiction and fact and creatures such as the ChupaCabra remain in many societies. The to the early development to vampirism (mostly its

177

mythology) and its belief in folklore in the obscurity of the process of decomposing the body after death , and the logic of preindustrial societies in their attempts to combine and justify this knowledge. Porphyria as we've described in this article is strongly linked to vampirism legends in 1985. This incident in 1985 received a lot of attention in the media, but was later dismissed.

If we look back the pages of the past and look back, we'll find that the mythical creature that we are familiar with today took origins in 1819, following The Vampyre was published. The Vampyre, a book written by John Polidori. The book and the tale contained in it are among the most popular and influential works on vampires during the nineteenth century. The basis for modern vampire is derived largely from the mythical nature of Bram Stoker's book Dracula published in the year 1897. The popularity of the novel by Bram Stocker created the unique vampire genre that we are familiar with and love reading and watching now. The vampire today is a prominent and constant character within the genre of horror. That brings us to vampires and vampirism, which has been a prominent feature in recent times.

The modern-day vampire is not a actual date of birth. The vampire that we are familiar today leaves little to the imagination, and very little authenticity to its fictitious or fictional character. In reality vampires and vampires are eternal in the natural world. This is a thing that hasn't changed over the years. This one fact alone raises several questions, one of the most important being the reason vampires were created. Since they are mythological in nature There isn't any evidence to prove the origins of the vampire species. Furthermore, theories on this topic make it impossible to understand the real nature and origins of this demon. There are some who believe that vampires originated from hell. Some think that the vampires were descendant of demons. It's difficult to determine or determine which of these is the truth. One thing that is commonly believed to be true (to an extent) is that folklore and vampires have existed for longer than humans have been around.

Vampirism is mentioned in the Bible as well as in ancient history

Vampirism is mentioned in the Bible

One of the legends surrounding vampire mythology has its origins found in the Holy Bible in the mention of a woman name of Lilith thought to have was in with Adam in the Garden of Eden with Adam. Lilith's inclusion in the Bible occurs only once (in the chapter of Isaiah 34:10) as well as once within the Jewish Torah. According to these references, Lilith was at one time identical to Adam. However, unlike Eve however, she wasn't dependent on Adam and could freely choose to be in Eden. According to the legend, Lilith and Adam argued often, mostly due to the fact that Lilith was a mate to Adam who demanded she lie down on her back for the sexual activity. In the wake of this failure by Lilith, Adam was angry with God and requested a soft woman to his image. This is why God prohibited Lilith and her children to eat fruit on the fruit tree that contained wisdom.

Infuriated by this decision After a while, Lilith began eating from the tree of knowledge. God gave Adam to punish her, only to discover that she had left in the garden prior to when he was able to get to her. After Lilith was able to escape from in the gardens, she picked up the practice to sleep with an alternate person every night.

After a while, Lilith got wind of the news about Adam's new bride, Eve. She was terrified about the possibility that Adam as well as Eve were going to have children. She also feared that Adam would have them pursue revenge. The fear, obsession and apprehension about Adam's children Adam led her to turn into a cannibal who ate, cursed and slain the children of Adam. Her sins changed into an eerie, terrifying winged beast. According to some religious organizations they believe this is the best and most rational explanation for why women are cursed by the ritual of bloodletting every month. Others believe that the myths and legends associated with vampires and vampirism have their roots from this story and also from the story of Cain Adam's son, who killed the brother of his Abel.

Vampirism in the early Egypt

If we examine other cultures, such as the old Egypt and ancient Egypt, we will see that vampires were common and an integral part of the early Egyptian beliefs. In the past, in Egypt the vampires were held in the same way as werewolves and cat folklore. Additionally, they were given the same importance as Egyptian gods. Additionally, vampires from early Egyptian culture were fierce and powerful in the sense that they were highly skilled. Within the tradition (ancient Egypt), Osiris and his brother were among the most well-known vampires. According to legends the vampires were adopted by those who believed in magic following the abandonment of their vampire parents by them. Their adoptive parents had two daughters of humankind: Nephytus and Isis. Osiris was a young man, got married to Isis and then became the king. As the king, he utilized the knowledge he acquired to instruct his people in Egypt how to cultivate the soil. Through Osiris the people of Egypt learned a lot about the practices of agriculture.

Afraid of his exasperating jealousy, Seth, Osiris' brother, started feeding on humans, and then creating more vampires in order to take over his brother and take the power of his own. Seth and his new vampires killed Osiris which made Seth the new Pharaoh. But, Horus was the son of Osiris collaborated together with Ra the sorcerer to create a curse for Seth and his vampires. The curse meant that vampires were unable to venture out into the sun or else they would be destroyed and end up dying. It is also the very first time of vampires being night-time creatures. In the time that Isis returned Osiris home, Osiris was tied to the netherworld, and was called Lord of the Underworld. Lord of the Underworld.

Vampirism in Greek mythology

Vampirism is also a factor in Greek mythology and culture. In Greek time vampires were believed to have different forms, and some were believed to be gods. According to popular and folklore beliefs, Hades was Osiris. Cain was known as Kronos/Cronus. Lilith was known as Circe. In the early days of Greek as well as Greek mythology Hades is the god of the Underworld. Cronus is known as the Titan god of the ages and time , and was also Zeus's father. Zeus. Because of a prophecy, which predicted his children would conquer and overthrow him Cronus consumed all his offspring's food, except for Zeus whom he saved. He was able to fight Kronos, his father. Kronos and his the brothers Hades, Poseidon and sent his father as well as other Titans to Tartaros which was run by goddess Hecate.

Additionally in Greek mythology Circe was one of the minor gods in Greek mythology. She is most commonly famous for her part in the epic Odyssey composed by Homer. Circe was the god of the magical (although her role in Greek mythology suggests it was she who was also a magician). Based on Greek legends, Circe was the one who invited Odysseus as well as her loved ones to the mansion of a place in the forests. She fed them well , but they drank their wine with a magical potion that transformed the swine into an animal. It was a practice she was famously known to indulge in after she snatched her adversaries or people who were against her. The mythology surrounding Circe is a part of Indian folklore, where she was known to feast on anyone who she turned into beasts.